Discl

Trademarks

Many of the designations used by manufacturers and sellers to distinguish their products are claimed as trademarks. Where those designations appear in this book, and the publisher was aware of a trademark claim, the designations appear as requested by the owner of the trademark. All other product names and services identified throughout this book are used in editorial fashion only and for the benefit of such companies with no intention of infringement of the trademark. No such use, or the use of any trade name, is intended to convey endorsement or other affiliation with this book.

1

Contents

Your feedback is invaluable to us

If you recently bought this book, we would love to hear from you!

You can do this by writing a review on Amazon (or the online store where you purchased this book) about your last purchase! As part of our continual service improvement process, we love to hear real client experiences and feedback.

How does it work?

To post a review on Amazon, just log in to your account and click on the Create Your Own Review button (under Customer Reviews) of the relevant product page. You can find examples of product reviews in Amazon. If you purchased from another online store, simply follow their procedures.

Java Web Developer

Java Web Developer 2617 Self Assessment & Interview Preparation Questions:

Self Assessment

1. What do you consider to be your professional Java Web Developer strengths? Give me a specific example using this attribute in the workplace

2. In what Java Web Developer ways are you trying to improve yourself?

3. Tell us about a time when you had to go above and beyond the call of duty in order to get a Java Web Developer job done

4. Give me a specific occasion in which you conformed to a Java Web Developer policy with which you did not agree

5. Can you recall a time when you were less than pleased with your Java Web Developer performance?

6. Give me an Java Web Developer example of an important goal that you h ad set in the past and tell me about your success in reaching it

7. Describe a Java Web Developer situation in which you were able to use persuasion to successfully convince someone to see things your way

8. What was the most useful criticism you ever received?

9. If there were one Java Web Developer area you've always wanted to improve upon, what would that be?

10. What Java Web Developer goal have you set for

yourself that you have successfully achieved?

Stress Management

1. What Java Web Developer kind of events cause you stress on the job?

2. People react differently when Java Web Developer job demands are constantly changing; how do you react?

3. How did you react when faced with constant time Java Web Developer pressure? Give an example

4. What was the most stressful Java Web Developer situation you have faced? How did you deal with it?

Problem Resolution

1. Describe a time in which you were faced with Java Web Developer problems or stresses which tested your coping skills. What did you do?

2. Describe a Java Web Developer situation where you had a conflict with another individual, and how you dealt with it. What was the outcome? How do you feel about it?

3. Tell us about a time when you identified a potential Java Web Developer problem and resolved the situation before it became serious

4. Sometimes we need to remain calm on the outside when we are really upset on the inside. Give an Java Web Developer example of a time that this happened to you

5. Give a specific Java Web Developer example of a time when you used good judgment and logic in solving a problem

6. Java Web Developer Problems occur in almost all work relationships. Describe a time when you had to cope with the resentment or hostility of a subordinate or co-worker

7. Sometimes the only Java Web Developer way to resolve a defense or conflict is through negotiation and compromise. Tell about a time when you were able to resolve a difficult situation by finding some common ground

8. Give an Java Web Developer example of a problem

which you faced on any job that you have had and tell how you went about solving it

9. Describe a time when you facilitated a creative Java Web Developer solution to a problem between two employees

10. Give an Java Web Developer example of when you 'went to the source' to address a conflict. Do you feel trust levels were improved as a result?

11. There is more than one Java Web Developer way to solve a problem. Give an example from your recent work experience that would illustrate this

12. Tell us about a recent Java Web Developer success you had with an especially difficult employee/co-worker

13. Some Java Web Developer problems require developing a unique approach. Tell about a time when you were able to develop a different problem-solving approach

14. Tell us about a Java Web Developer situation in which you had to separate the person from the issue when working to resolve issues

More questions about you

1. How do you feel about taking no for an answer?

2. What's the best Java Web Developer movie you've seen in the last year?

3. What is your biggest regret and why?

4. Give Java Web Developer examples of ideas you've had or implemented.

5. What magazines do you subscribe to?

6. List five Java Web Developer words that describe your character.

7. Tell me the Java Web Developer difference between good and exceptional.

8. What three Java Web Developer character traits would your friends use to describe you?

9. Tell me about your proudest achievement.

10. What do you do in your spare time?

11. What would be your ideal working Java Web Developer environment?

12. What Java Web Developer techniques and tools do you use to keep yourself organized?

13. What do you think of your previous Java Web Developer boss?

14. Why did you choose your major?

15. What do you ultimately want to become?

16. What do you look for in Java Web Developer terms of culture—structured or entrepreneurial?

17. How would you feel about working for someone who knows less than you?

18. What is your personal Java Web Developer mission statement?

19. How do you think I rate as an interviewer?

20. What is your favorite Java Web Developer memory from childhood?

21. Who has impacted you most in your Java Web Developer career and how?

22. If you had to choose one, would you consider yourself a big-Java Web Developer picture person or a detail-oriented person?

23. Tell me one thing about yourself you wouldn't want me to know.

24. Was there a person in your Java Web Developer career who really made a difference?

25. What is your greatest achievement outside of work?

26. What would you do if you won the lottery?

27. What are your lifelong Java Web Developer dreams?

28. What negative thing would your last Java Web Developer boss say about you?

29. What are you most proud of?

30. What Java Web Developer kind of car do you drive?

31. Who are your Java Web Developer heroes?

32. What is your greatest fear?

33. How would you describe your work Java Web Developer style?

34. What do you like to do for Java Web Developer fun?

35. What will you miss about your present/last Java Web Developer job?

36. What Java Web Developer kind of personality do you work best with and why?

37. What's the last Java Web Developer book you read?

38. What are three positive Java Web Developer character traits you don't have?

39. What's the most important thing you learned in school?

40. What are three positive Java Web Developer things your last boss would say about you?

41. There's no right or wrong answer, but if you could be anywhere in the Java Web Developer world right now, where would you be?

42. What are the Java Web Developer qualities of a good leader? A bad leader?

43. Who was your favorite Java Web Developer manager and why?

44. If you were interviewing someone for this position, what traits would you look for?

45. What do you like to do?

46. Do you think a Java Web Developer leader should be feared or liked?

Organizational

1. Describe a time when you had to make a difficult choice between your personal and professional Java Web Developer life

2. What do you do when your schedule is suddenly interrupted? Give an Java Web Developer example

3. How do you decide what gets top priority when scheduling your time?

4. Give me an Java Web Developer example of a project that best describes your organizational skills

Getting Started

1. What did you learn about _____?

2. How did you show it?

3. How did you solve the Java Web Developer problem?

4. Who Is Your Audience?

5. What Are Your Java Web Developer Questions?

6. What Java Web Developer information do you think potential clients would need to have to make an informed decision about whether they should get our product/services?

7. How can you use math Java Web Developer words to describe your experience?

8. How can you describe math?

9. If selected for this position, can you describe your Java Web Developer strategy for the first 90 days?

10. Would you give me an Java Web Developer example?

11. What Java Web Developer information are you/we going to use when solving a problem?

12. How would you go about establishing your credibility quickly with the Java Web Developer team?

13. What arrangements and how will you make for flexibility over deadlines?

14. Where do you see _____ at school?

15. How is this like something you have done before?

16. Can you elaborate on that Java Web Developer idea?

17. What changes did you have to make to solve a Java Web Developer problem?

18. How can you/we represent your/our thinking?

19. How do you know?

20. How would you explain _____ to a student in Grade ___?

21. How do you know if you have the wrong Java Web Developer questions?

22. What else would you like to find out about _____ ?

23. What do you see yourself doing within the first 30 days of this Java Web Developer job?

24. How long will it take for you to make a significant Java Web Developer contribution?

25. What Java Web Developer questions arose as you worked in the past 30 days?

26. How do you use these materials?

27. What prior Java Web Developer knowledge, experience, skills or qualifications do you you need for this job?

28. What do(es) _____ mean to you?

29. What Java Web Developer decisions did you make from a pattern that you discovered?

30. What did you learn today?

31. How do you feel about mathematics?

32. How can you show your thinking (e.g., Java Web Developer picture, model, number, sentence)?

33. What math Java Web Developer words did you use or learn?

34. How do you feel about _____ ?

35. What have you/we learned today?

36. How else might you have solved a recent Java Web Developer problem?

37. Have you/we found all the possibilities?

38. Which Java Web Developer way (e.g., picture, model, number, sentence) best shows what you know?

39. How would you/we explain what _____ just said, in your/our own Java Web Developer words?

40. Would you explain that further?

41. What would happen if you had a Java Web Developer team all set up and they are not getting along?

42. What did you do?

43. How do you know what Java Web Developer questions to ask?

44. What helped you accomplish _____?

45. What Java Web Developer strategy did you use?

46. Can you tell me more about that?

47. What other Java Web Developer problem have you solved recently?

48. What have you/we discovered about _____ while solving this Java Web Developer problem?

49. How Can YOU Use Java Web Developer Feedback?

50. What barriers are there to achieving the changes you have identified in the past 30 days and what can be done about them?

Presentation

1. Have you given presentations before?

2. How would you describe your Java Web Developer presentation style?

3. What has been your experience in giving presentations?

4. What Java Web Developer kinds of oral presentations have you made? How did you prepare for them? What challenges did you have?

5. Tell us about the most effective Java Web Developer presentation you have made. What was the topic? What made it difficult? How did you handle it?

6. How do you prepare for a Java Web Developer presentation to a group of technical experts in your field?

7. What Can You Do Now?

8. What has been your experience in making presentations or speeches?

Follow-up and Control

1. How did you keep track of delegated assignments?

2. How do you get Java Web Developer data for performance reviews?

3. What administrative paperwork do you have? Is it useful? Why/why not?

4. How do you evaluate the productivity/effectiveness of your subordinates?

5. How do you keep track of what your subordinates are doing?

Culture Fit

1. Do Java Web Developer heroes make moments or do moments make Java Web Developer heroes?

2. Fast, Good, and Cheap. Which two would you pick?

3. Are you incredibly passionate about solving the Java Web Developer problem that we are solving. Do you dream about it? Do you spend free time on it?

4. Pick two of our Java Web Developer company cultural values and provide an example for each where you've exemplified the value, preferably from your previous employment.

5. What other commitments do you have in your Java Web Developer life ... i.e. other jobs, school, family, community?

6. What would you fire a person for?

7. Are you the type to check your inbox on vacation?

8. Consider three Java Web Developer things – Humility, Hunger and Smarts. You may relate to one or all of these. Please tell me what you are the 'most-of' and what you are the 'least-of'?

9. What Java Web Developer environment do you thrive in the most and what drives your passion?

10. If you were starting a Java Web Developer company from scratch, what would you want your Java Web

Developer company's culture to be?

11. Why do you want to work for a startup when you could get a Java Web Developer job at a larger company, make more money and have a better work/life balance?

12. What does Java Web Developer culture mean to you?

13. What are your personal Java Web Developer values? And if you believe that your personal Java Web Developer values are aligned with the company's Java Web Developer values, please describe why.

14. What keeps you awake at night?

15. What specifically would you contribute to us during your first week of employment?

16. What does your ideal work Java Web Developer day look like?

17. What do you want from working with us? How can we help you accomplish that in this Java Web Developer role?

18. What are you passionate about outside of work?

19. Let's suppose that you found your dream Java Web Developer job with your ideal company that pays you well and has a great career path, title, benefits and perks. You have to start in 2 days and all you have to do is tell your boss what you'd want to do at this dream Java Web Developer job and you can have it - just like that. What

would you say that you'd like to do?

20. In your Java Web Developer opinion, what is leadership?

21. What do you see as your biggest Java Web Developer contribution to the world in 30 years?

Story

1. What is Your Experience with Work?

2. How do you reach your imaginary Java Web Developer world?

3. Who are your Java Web Developer key partners?

4. What barriers did you facd and how did you overcome them?

5. What would you share with your family about what you learned here today?

6. Did you feel you could tell your Java Web Developer story fully?

7. Will you play a game when you see it ?

8. Tell me about three major Java Web Developer life decisions that had you arrive here.

9. Tell me about a time when you were working on a Java Web Developer team and you disagreed with someone about how to do something. Tell me the whole story and how it was resolved.

10. Tell the Java Web Developer story of how you reached your conclusion in you most recent problem solving (steps you took, who was involved, whom you consulted, the level of time and effort involved)?

11. What do you suppose you found?

12. What Java Web Developer background information do you need to know to understand your story?

13. What restrictions do you have?

14. Whats your salary Java Web Developer history?

15. Tell me where you're from.

16. How do you manage to escape?

17. What can others take away and learn from your Java Web Developer story?

18. Who do you want to be?

19. How has your birth order made you who you are?

20. What advice do you have for us?

21. What's your Java Web Developer story?

22. Identify Java Web Developer examples from your past experience where you demonstrated those skills. How can you tell a story about your use of particular skills or knowledge?

23. What are your next Java Web Developer steps?

24. Can you tell me the Java Web Developer story of your prior success, challenges, and major responsibilities?

25. What are the aspects of your community that makes promoting healthy weight and Java Web Developer development in children particularly important, challenging or unique?

26. Where did you work?

27. Have you ever been hurt at work, or do you know someone who was?

28. How long have you been engaged in this process?

29. What would you tell a friend about today?

30. How did an Java Web Developer action plan help you tackle your work?

31. Which of your personal Java Web Developer experiences or memories is affecting your perceptions of the stories you tell?

32. How can you tell a Java Web Developer story about your use of particular skills or knowledge?

Innovation

1. Do you have the fortitude to challenge your Java Web Developer organization ALL the time?

2. Can you think of a disruptive Java Web Developer technology leading to a new market?

3. There are many Java Web Developer jobs in which well-established methods are typically followed. Give a specific example of a time when you tried some other method to do the job

4. Do you have a personal Java Web Developer example of market pull not generating a product – in other words do you need a product that doesnt exist, or a better product than the one that does exist?

5. There are many Java Web Developer jobs that require creative or innovative thinking. Give an example of when you had such a job and how you handled it

6. Tell us about a Java Web Developer suggestion you made to improve the way job processes/operations worked. What was the result?

7. How often have you come across an inventive new Java Web Developer product and thought, that seems obvious, why didnt I think of that?

8. Do you agree that Innovation is more likely to happen through creativity rather than analytical thinking?

9. The Java Web Developer pace of change and the

complexity of our relationship with technology are increasing. Do you agree or disagree?

10. If we are mature Java Web Developer business and are selling mature products, what is going to replace our products?

11. What can you do as a catalyst for Innovation?

12. What sort of Java Web Developer information would you need to obtain from an organisation in order to say what type of project organisation structure they used?

13. What have been some of your most creative Java Web Developer ideas?

14. Can you think of inventions that came about because of government Java Web Developer policy, legislation or regulations?

15. Tell us about a Java Web Developer problem that you solved in a unique or unusual way. What was the outcome? Were you satisfied with it?

16. Can you think of a Java Web Developer situation where innovation was required at work? What did you do in this Java Web Developer situation?

17. Can you think of inventions that resulted from a desire to help others?

18. Sometimes it is essential that we break out of the Java Web Developer routine, standardized way of doing things in order to complete the task. Give an example of

when you were able to successfully develop such a new approach

19. Describe a Java Web Developer situation when you demonstrated initiative and took action without waiting for direction. What was the outcome?

20. Can you think of an incremental innovation?

21. When was the last time that you thought 'outside of the box' and how did you do it?

22. Which innovations would you describe as predominantly arising from Java Web Developer technology push and which from market pull?

23. Describe a time when you came up with a creative Java Web Developer solution/idea/project/report to a problem in your past work

24. What new or unusual Java Web Developer ideas have you developed on your job? How did you develop them? What was the result? Did you implement them?

25. Can you think of a Java Web Developer situation where innovation was required at work?

26. What innovative Java Web Developer procedures have you developed? How did you develop them? Who was involved? Where did the ideas come from?

27. If you have a proposed project topic, would different players define Java Web Developer success in the same or different ways?

28. Describe the most creative work-related project which you have carried out

29. What do you think of the statement: a Java Web Developer company that has a structured environment (traditional) will lack employees with innovation skills?

30. Describe something that you have implemented at work. What were the Java Web Developer steps used to implement this?

31. Can you think of inventions that took the opportunity offered by a new material, Java Web Developer technology or manufacturing process?

32. To what Java Web Developer degree did you involve customer service agents in the design of an innovation?

33. Can you think of another Java Web Developer example of a radical innovation?

Variety

1. When was the last time you were in a crisis? What was the Java Web Developer situation? How did you react?

2. Which of your Java Web Developer jobs had the most rapid change? How did you feel about it?

3. How many Java Web Developer projects do you work on at once? Please describe

4. When was the last time you made a Java Web Developer key decision on the spur of the moment? What was the reason and result?

Persuasion

1. What do you know about the lives of women in the late 18th century?

2. What do you believe you owe your family?

3. What would you consider to be a terrific place to go for a vacation?

4. Tell us about a time when you were able to successfully influence another person

5. Tell us about a time when you had to convince someone in authority about your Java Web Developer ideas. How did it work out?

6. On what matters in your Java Web Developer life would you be open to family opinions or persuasion?

7. Describe a Java Web Developer situation where you were able to use persuasion to successfully convince someone to see things your way

8. In selling an Java Web Developer idea, it is sometimes useful to use metaphors, analogies, or stories to make your point. Give a recent example of when you were able to successfully do that

9. You are introduced to three new people and miss one of the names. What do you do?

10. How is your offer most persuasive?

11. Advertise a Java Web Developer movie. What

elements would you emphasize to create print or radio campaigns?

12. Describe a time when you were able to convince a skeptical or resistant Java Web Developer customer to purchase a project or utilize your services

13. To what extent are Java Web Developer education, economic stability, family background, temperament, race, religion, ethnicity, or language important to you?

14. In working with other Java Web Developer team members, how might your preferences get in the way or block the success of the Java Web Developer team?

15. What Java Web Developer questions could you raise that would get others to want to hire you?

16. What Java Web Developer jobs are your primary preferences most often associated with?

17. Have you seen any reference to yourself on radio or TV or in the newspaper?

18. What are your primary Java Web Developer personality preferences?

19. Have you ever had to persuade a peer or Java Web Developer manager to accept an idea that you knew they would not like? Describe the resistance you met and how you overcame it

20. Tell us about a time when you used your Java Web Developer leadership ability to gain support for what

initially had strong opposition

21. Suppose you must implement an unpopular Java Web Developer policy at work. You want to persuade your employees that the Java Web Developer policy is a positive change. Should you present one side of the issue or both sides?

22. Tell us about a time when you used Java Web Developer facts and reason to persuade someone to accept your recommendation

23. What elements would you emphasize to create print or radio campaigns?

24. Think about your Java Web Developer character. What contemporary songs would you identify with?

25. Describe a Java Web Developer situation in which you were able to positively influence the actions of others in a desired direction

26. How do you get a peer or Java Web Developer colleague to accept one of your ideas?

27. What do the Java Web Developer tasks look like from your point of view?

28. What will you learn?

29. Why should people believe you?

30. Which lines, Java Web Developer ideas, and/or actions resonate with you or repulse you?

31. Which actors and actresses are different from the Java Web Developer way you envisioned them?

32. Given your type, what about your preferences is likely to make you personally effective?

33. You are telephoning somebody about something that is important to you. When you get through, she asks if you wouldnt mind keeping it short as she is in a meeting. Do you?

34. Have you ever had to persuade a Java Web Developer group to accept a proposal or idea? How did you go about doing it? What was the result?

Analytical Thinking

1. Give me a specific Java Web Developer example of a time when you used good judgment and logic in solving a problem

2. What Java Web Developer resources, human and other, remain untapped in our organization?

3. Which of our Managerial Competencies most support your personal Java Web Developer development goals?

4. What's the connection between hands and the ocean?

5. Do you agree with author James Fixx, who asserts, In solving puzzles, a self-assured Java Web Developer attitude is half the battle?

6. Tell us about your experience in past Java Web Developer jobs that required you to be especially alert to details while doing the task involved

7. Do you know what the Java Web Developer outcome should be after you follow instructions?

8. What do you do when the patterns break down?

9. Ever see the face of someone you know in a potato chip?

10. What is critical thinking and analytical thinking?

11. What is your approach to solving Java Web Developer problems?

12. What do you think Tom Peters means when he says, If you have gone a whole week without being disobedient, you are doing yourself and your Java Web Developer organization a disservice?

13. Describe the project or Java Web Developer situation which best demonstrates your analytical abilities. What was your role?

14. How can we maximize the investment in your training, after the training?

15. Tell us about a time when you had to analyze Java Web Developer information and make a recommendation. What kind of thought process did you go through? What was your reasoning behind your decision?

16. What is your evaluation of the educational training at secondary level in our country?

17. In your current Java Web Developer job role, what energizes you?

18. What Java Web Developer techniques do you know of to stimulate free association or brainstorming?

19. Give me an Java Web Developer example of when you took a risk to achieve a goal. What was the outcome?

20. What are you looking at that no one else can see?

21. Should spent nuclear fuel be reprocessed?

22. What is the greatest Java Web Developer contribution you can make to this organization?

23. How does this activity we're doing right now relate to thinking?

24. What rules do you feel should be changed?

25. How did you go about making the changes (step by step)? Answer in Java Web Developer depth or detail such as 'What were you thinking at that point?' or 'Tell me more about meeting with that person', or 'Lead me through your decision process'

26. What happens when you are called upon to make a statement on the spot, to make a Java Web Developer decision without having all the facts, to solve a problem that will only be exacerbated by delay?

27. Developing and using a detailed Java Web Developer procedure is often very important in a job. Tell about a time when you needed to develop and use a detailed Java Web Developer procedure to successfully complete a project

28. How does this activity we're doing right now relate to learning?

29. Do you ask yourself after every interaction with the Java Web Developer team, Have I left them feeling stronger and more capable than before?

30. Tell us about a Java Web Developer job or setting where great precision to detail was required to complete a task. How did you handle that situation?

31. Relate a specific Java Web Developer instance when you found it necessary to be precise in your in order to complete the job

Communication

1. Tell us about a recent successful experience in making a Java Web Developer speech or presentation. How did you prepare? What obstacles did you face? How did you handle them?

2. Describe a Java Web Developer situation where you felt you had not communicated well. How did you correct the Java Web Developer situation?

3. Tell me about a successful Java Web Developer presentation you gave and why you think it was a hit.

4. How do you keep subordinates informed about Java Web Developer information that affects their jobs?

5. Tell me about a time when you had to rely on written Java Web Developer communication to get your ideas across to your team.

6. Tell us about an experience in which you had to speak up in order to be sure that other people knew what you thought or felt

7. Tell us about a time when you had to present complex Java Web Developer information. How did you ensure that the other person understood?

8. Have you had to 'sell' an Java Web Developer idea to your co-workers, classmates or group? How did you do it? Did they 'buy' it?

9. Describe a time when you were the Java Web

Developer resident technical expert. What did you do to make sure everyone was able to understand you?

10. Give me an Java Web Developer example of a time when you had to explain something fairly complex to a frustrated client. How did you handle this delicate situation?

11. Tell us me about a Java Web Developer situation when you had to speak up (be assertive) in order to get a point across that was important to you

12. Tell us about a time when you and your current/ previous supervisor disagreed but you still found a Java Web Developer way to get your point across

13. Give me an Java Web Developer example of a time when you were able to successfully communicate with another person, even when that individual may not have personally liked you

14. How have you persuaded people through a Java Web Developer document you prepared?

15. What Java Web Developer kinds of writing have you done? How do you prepare written communications?

16. Describe a Java Web Developer situation in which you were able to effectively 'read' another person and guide your actions by your understanding of their individual needs or values

17. What have you done to improve your verbal Java Web Developer communication skills?

18. What are the most challenging documents you have done? What Java Web Developer kinds of proposals have your written?

19. Tell us about a time when you had to use your verbal Java Web Developer communication skills in order to get a point across that was important to you

20. What Java Web Developer challenges have occurred while you were coordinating work with other units, departments, and/or divisions?

21. Describe a time when you were able to effectively communicate a difficult or unpleasant Java Web Developer idea to a superior

22. Give me an Java Web Developer example of a time when you were able to successfully communicate with another person, even when that individual may not have personally liked you, or vice versa

23. Tell us about a time when you were particularly effective in a talk you gave or a Java Web Developer seminar you taught

24. Describe a Java Web Developer situation when you were able to strengthen a relationship by communicating effectively. What made your communication effective?

25. How do you go about explaining a complex technical Java Web Developer problem to a person who does not understand technical jargon? What approach do you take in communicating with people?

26. Have you ever had to 'sell' an Java Web Developer idea to your co-workers or group? How did you do it? Did they 'buy' it?

27. Give me an Java Web Developer example of a time when you were able to successfully persuade someone to see things your way at work.

28. Tell us me about a time in which you had to use your written Java Web Developer communication skills in order to get an important point across

29. How do you keep your Java Web Developer manager informed about what is being done in your work area?

30. Describe the most significant written Java Web Developer document, report or presentation which you had to complete

31. What Java Web Developer kinds of communication situations cause you difficulty? Give an example

Building Relationships

1. How would your best friend describe you to someone you have never met?

2. How will we communicate with each other?

3. What is something you are excited about this year?

4. If you were the weather, how would you describe yourself?

5. Give a specific Java Web Developer example of a time when you had to address an angry customer. What was the problem and what was the outcome? How would you asses your role in diffusing the situation?

6. What is one thing you are really good at outside of work?

7. What super-Java Web Developer power would you most like to have?

8. If you opened a restaurant, what would it be like?

9. If you were president, what new law would you make?

10. Who are the individuals that have considerable influence with other people in our current or previous Java Web Developer organization?

11. What are the Java Web Developer qualities of an effective mentor?

12. Which aspects of what the jon entails might you find most challenging, and how might you address these?

13. A simple question goes to the very heart of your work in winning Java Web Developer resources and support: how do you ask people for something?

14. What do you do (your behaviors, Java Web Developer actions, feelings) that indicates you are loyal?

15. What is something you have done to get an A in class?

16. How do you want to change over the next 5-10 Java Web Developer years?

17. Tell us about a time when you built rapport quickly with someone under difficult Java Web Developer conditions

18. If you could have dinner with one person (dead or alive) who would it be?

19. If they made a Java Web Developer movie of your life what actor would play you?

20. Why are the numbers on a calculator and a phone reversed?

21. When you were a kid, what did you want to be when you grew up?

22. How does one build interpersonal Java Web Developer relationships?

23. How do you sustain interpersonal Java Web Developer relationships with key stakeholders?

24. What strategies have you utilised to establish strong Java Web Developer relationships with peers?

25. What is the strangest thing you have ever eaten?

26. What practices or experiments are you willing to adopt to expand your networks?

27. How does one go about the Java Web Developer task of relationship building?

28. What is something you are worried about this year?

29. What are the handles for corn on the cob called?

30. Was there an peer whom you especially enjoyed spending time with?

31. Are you consistent, predictable, open and honest?

32. It is very important to build good Java Web Developer relationships at work but sometimes it doesn't always work. If you can, tell about a time when you were not able to build a successful relationship with a difficult person

33. Are you a morning person, or a night person?

34. What would you most like to be remembered for?

35. What does it mean to be responsive to all colleagues?

36. Where would you like to build your Java Web Developer relationships or extend your network?

37. If you lost your sense of smell but could only pick 3 Java Web Developer things that you would still be able to smell, what 3 smells would you pick?

38. What are three or four Java Web Developer qualities you have that are going to help you be a great mentor?

39. Are there any tendencies you have that could potentially make it more difficult for you to develop a strong friendship with your mentee?

40. What place in the Java Web Developer world would you most like to visit?

41. Who influences your work and whom do you have influence on?

42. Do you know what we are supposed to be doing right now?

43. How many negative Java Web Developer relationships do you have at work?

44. What is your biggest Java Web Developer weakness you have had to overcome?

45. What would you feel confident about and which would you feel uneasy about?

46. What do you expect will change for your mentee as a result of his or her Java Web Developer relationship with you?

47. What is your biggest strength that will help you in this Java Web Developer job?

48. Which bad habits of other people drive you crazy?

49. What, in your Java Web Developer opinion, are the key ingredients in guiding and maintaining successful business relationships? Give examples of how you made these work for you

50. Do people agree with the policies in your workplace?

Performance Management

1. Tell us about a time when you had to tell a Java Web Developer staff member that you were dissatisfied with his or her work

2. How do you handle a subordinate whose work is not up to expectations?

3. Tell us about a time when you had to use your authority to get something done. Where there any negative consequences?

4. How often do you discuss a subordinate's Java Web Developer performance with him/her? Give an example

5. Tell us about a training Java Web Developer program that you have developed or enhanced

6. What have you done to develop the Java Web Developer skills of your staff?

7. There are times when people need extra help. Give an Java Web Developer example of when you were able to provide that support to a person with whom you worked

8. Tell us about a time when you had to take disciplinary Java Web Developer action with someone you supervised

9. How do you handle Java Web Developer performance reviews? Tell me about a difficult one

10. How do you coach a subordinate to develop a new

Java Web Developer skill?

11. When do you give positive Java Web Developer feedback to people? Tell me about the last time you did. Give an example of how you handle the need for constructive criticism with a subordinate or peer

12. Give an Java Web Developer example of how you have been successful at empowering either a person or a group of people into accomplishing a task

13. Give an Java Web Developer example of a time when you helped a staff member accept change and make the necessary adjustments to move forward. What were the change/transition skills that you used

14. Tell us about a specific Java Web Developer development plan that you created and carried out with one or more of your employees What was the specific situation? What were the components of the Java Web Developer development plan? What was the outcome?

Interpersonal Skills

1. Do you have the confidence that you desire?

2. How did you feel?

3. Do you have any Java Web Developer questions of us about this position?

4. What might your current colleagues say about you and the Java Web Developer way you relate to others?

5. Did anything make you laugh today?

6. Have you ever been called a worrywart?

7. What does your Java Web Developer brain contain?

8. What does personal responsibility mean to you?

9. Do you have a plan?

10. At least how many people a week do you communicate with?

11. What have you done in past situations to contribute toward a teamwork Java Web Developer environment?

12. Self-regard is the ability to respect and accept oneself as you are. In which areas are you satisfied or dissatisfied?

13. How do you feel today?

14. Tell us how you have handled past work situations that required confidentiality. How might that Java Web Developer procedure impact this office?

15. If 1 = the worst and 10 = the best, how would you rate your sleep on average these days?

16. What Java Web Developer kind of supervision have you had in the past and how have you responded to it?

17. This Java Web Developer office is many times all things to all people. How do you see your skills and personality fitting into that expectation?

18. Question your own defensiveness. What Java Web Developer situation makes you upset?

19. Think of the person who knows you best; a person who knows both good and bad Java Web Developer things about your personality. What might they say about you and the way you relate to others?

20. What gives you strength?

21. Do you feel rested or not rested when you wake up?

22. Are the beliefs that you have about yourself TRUE or FALSE?

23. What are the most important Java Web Developer things in your life?

24. Spend a few minutes thinking about what the best Java Web Developer day of your life would be like. Then tell a story describing in detail everything about that Java Web Developer day. What makes this one Java Web Developer day the best Java Web Developer day of your life?

25. Tell us about the most difficult or frustrating individual that you've ever had to work with, and how you managed to work with them

26. Are you doing what needs to be done to meet your Java Web Developer goals?

27. Describe a Java Web Developer situation in which you were able to effectively 'read' another person and guide your actions by your understanding of their needs and values

28. Bad Java Web Developer things happen to people all the time in our world. What if they were to happen to you?

29. How would you handle Java Web Developer questions that go beyond your knowledge?

30. What makes one Java Web Developer day the best Java Web Developer day of your life?

31. What is troubling you?

32. Describe a recent unpopular Java Web Developer decision you made and what the result was

33. What causes you to lose your cool?

34. In which areas are you satisfied or dissatisfied?

35. Do you nap during the Java Web Developer day?

36. What have you done in the past to contribute toward a teamwork Java Web Developer environment?

37. Which code of practice do you use to review your Java Web Developer performance?

38. How many times have you tried to communicate with an Java Web Developer organization by phone and been left feeling really frustrated?

39. Without taking the Java Web Developer problem on yourself, whom would you help and what Java Web Developer problems would you help them solve?

40. What do you enjoy doing?

41. What is the funniest thing that has ever happened to you?

42. What would you save in the event of a disaster such as a fire or a flood?

43. How many Java Web Developer hours do you sleep if you add them all up, even if they are interrupted?

44. How do you see your Java Web Developer skills and personality fitting into our organization?

45. What is your understanding of the Java Web Developer word teamwork and how you have been involved with that process on the job or in other settings. How might teamwork (or lack of it) affect an office setting?

46. What do you do well?

47. How would you characterize my interpersonal Java Web Developer skills?

48. What keeps you going and/or gives you hope?

49. Who is one of the funniest people you know?

50. Evaluate your progress towards your Java Web Developer goals. Are you doing what needs to be done to meet your Java Web Developer goals?

51. If you were forced to live under a different political régime that is very different from that which you know, what would be most important to you?

Initiative

1. Give me Java Web Developer examples of projects/ tasks you started on your own

2. What Java Web Developer kinds of things really get your excited?

3. How did you get work assignments at your most recent employer?

4. Give me an Java Web Developer example of when you had to go above and beyond the call of duty in order to get a job done

5. What Java Web Developer sorts of things did you do at school that were beyond expectations?

6. What Java Web Developer sorts of projects did you generate that required you to go beyond your job description?

7. What changes did you develop at your most recent employer?

8. Give some Java Web Developer instances in which you anticipated problems and were able to influence a new direction

Listening

1. When you face a Java Web Developer problem, what do you do?

2. When is listening important on your Java Web Developer job? When is listening difficult?

3. How can you empower and motivate the Java Web Developer team?

4. What did you want to do when you graduated?

5. Give an Java Web Developer example of a time when you made a mistake because you did not listen well to what someone had to say

6. How can you determine how well you listen?

7. What do you do when you think someone is not listening to you?

8. When you are a listener, how can you encourage a speaker?

9. When is listening important in your Java Web Developer job?

10. Do you have good vocabulary Java Web Developer skills?

11. What Java Web Developer challenges have you faced while listening?

12. When is listening important on your Java Web Developer job?

13. Please give me an Java Web Developer example of a time when youve demonstrated good listening skills?

14. What do you do to show people that you are listening to them?

15. What do you do to show people that you are listing to them?

16. Do you think there is a Java Web Developer difference between hearing and listening?

17. Can you make a simple Java Web Developer story based on a picture?

18. Are you listening, involving and encouraging?

19. How often do you have to rely on Java Web Developer information you have gathered from others when talking to them? What kinds of problems have you had? What happened?

20. How do you give Java Web Developer staff motivating feedback?

21. Do you ask eliciting Java Web Developer questions such as What do you mean?

22. Are you good at listening?

23. How do you acquire a second language?

24. How can you know the gestures you use are effective?

25. How do you know when someone is listening to you?

Setting Priorities

1. When given an important assignment, how do you approach it?

2. Were there times that you could have used more efficiently?

3. How do you currently spend your time?

4. All of us have these barriers. Name some barriers to effective time Java Web Developer management in your life. Are these barriers that can be removed or avoided?

5. How do you manage your time?

6. What strategies do you use to priorities?

7. Have you ever been overloaded with work? How do you keep track of work so that it gets done on time?

8. How do you schedule your time?

9. What Java Web Developer kind of measuring stick do you use to distinguish the difference between activities that are essential versus things which are nonessential?

10. Which of your Java Web Developer activities was really important?

11. What Java Web Developer questions can you ask yourself to help you prioritize your tasks?

12. Do you spend too much time on some Java Web Developer activities?

13. How do you set priorities?

14. Are you a morning person, or do you have more energy in the evening?

15. How do you decided what to buy?

16. Consider your energy level. Are you a morning person, or do you have more energy in the evening?

17. What Java Web Developer kinds of discussion do you remember about finances before or soon after your marriage?

18. What are some Java Web Developer steps you take to overcome procrastination?

19. How do you determine you have a critical Java Web Developer problem?

20. Is saying no to peoples requests of you a different thing to do?

Relate Well

1. Tell us about a time when you were forced to make an unpopular Java Web Developer decision

2. Describe a Java Web Developer situation where you had to use conflict management skills

3. Describe a Java Web Developer situation where you had to use confrontation skills

4. What would your co-workers (or Java Web Developer staff) stay is the most frustrating thing about your communications with them?

5. Give me an Java Web Developer example of a time when a company policy or action hurt people. What, if anything, did you do to mitigate the negative consequences to people?

6. How do you typically deal with conflict? Can you give me an Java Web Developer example?

Problem Solving

1. Have you ever been caught unaware by a Java Web Developer problem or obstacles that you had not foreseen? What happened?

2. What are some of the Java Web Developer problems you have faced; such as between business development and project leaders, between one department and another, between you and your peers? How did you recognize that they were there?

3. If you were to build a Java Web Developer product that addresses the problem we are trying to solve, what would it look like?

4. If you had to automate the Java Web Developer job for which you are applying, how would you do it?

5. What important Java Web Developer truth do very few people agree with you on?

6. Describe the most difficult working Java Web Developer relationship you've had with an individual. What specific actions did you take to improve the Java Web Developer relationship? What was the outcome?

7. You are interviewing for Java Web Developer job X ... suppose we instead offered you Java Web Developer job Y (unrelated to current area of proficiency), what are the first 3 things you would do to ensure your success in that role?

8. If you were the CEO of your last Java Web Developer company, what are 3 things you would of changed?

9. Where everyone sees a Java Web Developer problem, what do you see?

10. If you could design a Java Web Developer business to disrupt ours, what would that Java Web Developer business look like?

11. Who are you going to call to tell about our (amazing new) Java Web Developer product, and what will you ask them?

12. What is my Java Web Developer company doing wrong and how would you fix it?

13. You're in the airport about to board a plane to go to Singapore and you realize that you lost the Java Web Developer contact information of the person you were going to visit and don't have enough money to stay in a hotel or get another airplane ticket—what's your plan?

14. Can you tell me what your understanding of what our Java Web Developer company does?

15. Describe the most challenging Java Web Developer situation you had experienced in your last job and how did you overcome it?

16. When was the last time something came up in a meeting that was not covered in the plan? What did you do? What were the Java Web Developer results of your judgment?

17. Beatles or Stones? And why?

18. Tell us about a time when you did something completely different from the plan and/or assignment. Why? What happened?

19. If you had $100,000 to build your own Java Web Developer business, what would you do and why?

20. Give me an Java Web Developer example of a situation where you had difficulties with a team member. What, if anything, did you do to resolve the difficulties?

21. Why would Java Web Developer clients and prospects want to use our product/ service?

22. Tell me about some typical Java Web Developer activities that you completed in your last job that made you feel excited, were in your flow and, afterwards, made you feel emotionally stronger?

Basic interview question

1. Why do you want this Java Web Developer job?

2. What's your ideal Java Web Developer company?

3. What can you do for us that other Java Web Developer candidates can't?

4. What do you know about this Java Web Developer industry?

5. Do you have any Java Web Developer questions for me?

6. When were you most satisfied in your Java Web Developer job?

7. What are your weaknesses?

8. Tell me about yourself.

9. Why should we hire you?

10. Why are you leaving your present Java Web Developer job?

11. Where would you like to be in your Java Web Developer career five years from now?

12. What attracted you to this Java Web Developer company?

13. What did you like least about your last Java Web

Developer job?

14. What were the responsibilities of your last position?

15. What are your Java Web Developer strengths?

16. Behavioral Java Web Developer interview questions

17. What do you know about our Java Web Developer company?

Like-ability

1. Tell us about a time when you were able to build a successful Java Web Developer relationship with a difficult person.

2. Have you ever had Java Web Developer difficulty getting along with a co-worker? How did you handle the situation and what was the outcome?

3. Some people are difficult to work with. Tell us about a time when you encountered such a person. How did you handle it?

4. Tell us about a Java Web Developer situation in which you became frustrated or impatient when dealing with a coworker. What did you do? What was the outcome?

5. Having an understanding of the other person's Java Web Developer perspective is crucial in dealing with customers. Give us an example of a time when you achieved success through attaining insight into the other person's Java Web Developer perspective.

6. On occasion we may be faced with a Java Web Developer situation that has escalated to become a confrontation. If you have had such an experience, tell me how you handled it. What was the outcome? Would you do anything differently today?

7. Give us an Java Web Developer example of how you have been able to develop a close, positive relationship with one of your customers.

8. We don't always make Java Web Developer decisions

that everyone agrees with. Give us an example of an unpopular decision you have made. How did you communicate the decision and what was the outcome?

9. It is important to remain composed at work and to maintain a positive outlook. Give us a specific Java Web Developer example of when you were able to do this.

10. Describe a particularly trying Java Web Developer customer complaint or resistance you had to handle. How did you react and what was the outcome?

11. In working with people, we find that what works with one person does not work with another. Therefore, we have to be flexible in our Java Web Developer style of relating to others. Give us a specific example of when you had to vary your work Java Web Developer style with a particular individual. How did it work out?

12. Tell us about a time when you needed someone's cooperation to complete a Java Web Developer task and the person was uncooperative. What did you do? What was the outcome?

13. How would you describe your Java Web Developer management style? How do you think your subordinates perceive you?

14. Many Java Web Developer jobs are team-oriented where a work group is the key to success. Give us an example of a time when you worked on a team to complete a project. How did it work? What was the outcome?

15. Give us an Java Web Developer example of how you establish an atmosphere at work where others feel comfortable in communicating their ideas, feelings and concerns.

16. There are times when people need extra Java Web Developer assistance with difficult projects. Give us an example of when you offered Java Web Developer assistance to someone with whom you worked.

17. Describe a time when you weren't sure what a Java Web Developer customer wanted. How did you handle the situation?

18. Tell us about a Java Web Developer job where the atmosphere was the easiest for you to get along and function well. Describe the qualities of that work environment.

Career Development

1. Whats the last Java Web Developer book you read?

2. What are your interest?

3. What is your greatest Java Web Developer weakness?

4. What do you do in your spare time?

5. Do you think a Java Web Developer leader should be feared or liked?

6. Who has impacted you most in your Java Web Developer career and how?

7. What Java Web Developer kind of personality do you work best with and why?

8. How can YOU monitor your Java Web Developer data?

9. What would you think about a Java Web Developer career that required a great deal of travel?

10. What is your greatest Java Web Developer failure, and what did you learn from it?

11. Did you think about what the Java Web Developer outcome should be?

12. What would be your ideal working Java Web Developer situation?

13. Why was there a Java Web Developer gap in your employment between insert date and insert date?

14. Related occupation: Are there other Java Web Developer career fields/occupations that look like a good match for you?

15. How would you feel about working for someone who knows less than you?

16. What magazines do you subscribe to?

17. What are your lifelong Java Web Developer dreams?

18. Whats your availability?

19. What is your greatest fear?

20. What Java Web Developer types of careers fit your skills and interest?

21. What do you look for in Java Web Developer terms of culture -structured or entrepreneurial?

22. What do your reports reflect?

23. If I were to ask your last supervisor to provide you additional training or Java Web Developer exposure, what would she suggest?

24. What would you do if you won the lottery?

25. Who reviews your Java Web Developer data?

26. Give me an Java Web Developer example of a time you did something wrong. How did you handle it?

27. How would you describe your work Java Web Developer style?

28. What Java Web Developer techniques and tools do you use to keep yourself organized?

29. Who are your collaborators?

30. What would be your ideal working Java Web Developer environment?

31. How do you feel about taking no for an answer?

32. What are your Java Web Developer skills?

33. What Java Web Developer kind of car do you drive?

34. What are three positive Java Web Developer character traits you dont have?

35. Have you ever been on a Java Web Developer team where someone was not pulling their weight?

36. What negative thing would your last Java Web Developer boss say about you?

37. Worried Youre In A Dead-End Java Web Developer Job?

38. What do you like to do?

39. What do you see yourself doing 5 or 10 Java Web Developer years from now?

40. How would you define a positive work Java Web Developer environment?

41. What are you looking for in Java Web Developer terms of career development?

42. What were the responsibilities of your last position?

43. What are some aspects of your present Java Web Developer job that you enjoy / dislike?

44. What do you ultimately want to become?

45. What is your greatest achievement outside of work?

46. What is your plan for competency attainment?

47. Why should I hire you?

48. How do you prepare for the Java Web Developer career?

49. What is your personal Java Web Developer mission statement?

50. How do you think I rate as an interviewer?

51. Are you a Java Web Developer team player?

52. If you were interviewing someone for this position, what traits would you look for?

53. What does your appearance say about you?

54. If you could choose one superhero Java Web Developer power, what would it be and why?

55. What was the last project you headed up, and what was its Java Web Developer outcome?

56. Why did you apply to this position?

57. What will you miss about your present/last Java Web Developer job?

58. What irritates you about other people, and how do you deal with it?

59. Whats the most difficult Java Web Developer decision youve made in the last two years and how did you come to that Java Web Developer decision?

60. What else besides your schooling and experience qualify you for this Java Web Developer job?

61. Whats the most important thing you learned in school?

62. What is your Java Web Developer Career Goal?

63. What do you want to be?

64. Whats the best Java Web Developer movie youve

seen in the last year?

65. Who do you serve?

66. What are your interests?

67. Identify what is unique or special about you. How have you gone above and beyond the call of duty?

68. What are three positive Java Web Developer things your last boss would say about you?

69. What Java Web Developer kind of goals would you have in mind if you got this job?

70. How do you handle working with people who annoy you?

71. What assignment was too difficult for you, and how did you resolve the Java Web Developer issue?

72. Who was your favorite Java Web Developer manager and why?

73. Whos your Java Web Developer mentor?

74. Why did you choose your major?

75. How would you feel about a Java Web Developer job that required you to move on a regular basis?

76. What is your biggest regret and why?

77. What do you know about this Java Web Developer industry?

78. What do you like to do for Java Web Developer fun?

79. What are you looking for in Java Web Developer terms of career development?

80. How would you define a positive work Java Web Developer environment?

81. If you found out your Java Web Developer company was doing something against the law, like fraud, what would you do?

82. Was there a person in your Java Web Developer career who really made a difference?

83. How long will it take you to make a Java Web Developer contribution?

84. What three Java Web Developer character traits would your friends use to describe you?

85. How do you want to improve yourself in the next year?

86. What do you think of your previous Java Web Developer boss?

87. Java Web Developer Education and/or training after high school: What colleges or training programs did you attend to prepare for your preferred occupations?

88. What specific Java Web Developer steps did you take and what was your particular contribution?

89. What Java Web Developer education is required for your chosen career?

90. What is your favorite Java Web Developer memory from childhood?

91. Have you ever been on a Java Web Developer team where someone was not pulling their own weight?

92. What was the last project you led, and what was its Java Web Developer outcome?

93. What Java Web Developer qualities do you feel a successful manager should have?

94. Can you describe a time when your work was criticized?

95. Whats your ideal Java Web Developer company?

96. How have you gone above and beyond the call of duty?

97. If you had to choose one, would you consider yourself a big-Java Web Developer picture person or a detail-oriented person?

98. How much do outside influences play a Java Web Developer role in your job performance?

99. What was the most difficult Java Web Developer period in your life, and how did you deal with it?

100. In thinking about your Java Web Developer future, you must consider whats important to you in your daily life. What would you think about a career that required a great deal of travel?

101. What were your Java Web Developer bosses strengths/weaknesses?

102. What Java Web Developer questions havent I asked you?

103. Have you ever had a conflict with a Java Web Developer boss or professor?

104. Theres no right or wrong answer, but if you could be anywhere in the Java Web Developer world right now, where would you be?

105. What do you look for in Java Web Developer terms of culture -- structured or entrepreneurial?

106. What Java Web Developer kind of goals would you have in mind if you got this job?

Caution

1. Tell us me about a Java Web Developer situation when it was important for you to pay attention to details. How did you handle it?

2. Have you ever worked in a Java Web Developer situation where the rules and guidelines were not clear? Tell me about it. How did you feel about it? How did you react?

3. Some people consider themselves to be 'big Java Web Developer picture people' and others are 'detail oriented'. Which are you? Give an example of a time when you displayed this

4. Tell us me about a time when you demonstrated too much initiative?

Sound Judgment

1. We work with a great deal of confidential Java Web Developer information. Describe how you would have handled sensitive Java Web Developer information in a past work experience. What strategies would you utilize to maintain confidentiality when pressured by others?

2. Give me an Java Web Developer example of when you were able to meet the personal and professional demands in your life yet still maintained a healthy balance

3. If you were interviewing for this position what would you be looking for in the applicants?

4. Give me an Java Web Developer example of a time in which you had to be relatively quick in coming to a decision

5. Describe a Java Web Developer situation when you had to exercise a significant amount of self-control

6. When have you had to produce Java Web Developer results without sufficient guidelines? Give an example

7. Give me an Java Web Developer example of when you were responsible for an error or mistake. What was the outcome? What, if anything, would you do differently?

Salary and Remuneration

1. What salary are you seeking?

2. If I were to give you this salary you Java Web Developer requested but let you write your job description for the next year, what would it say?

3. What's your salary Java Web Developer history?

Strategic Planning

1. Describe what Java Web Developer steps/methods you have used to define/identify a vision for your unit/position

2. In your current or former position, what were your long and short-Java Web Developer term goals?

3. Tell us about a time when you anticipated the Java Web Developer future and made changes to current responsibilities/operations to meet Java Web Developer future needs

4. How do you see your Java Web Developer job relating to the overall goals of the organization?

Negotiating

1. What is your walk away point?

2. Have you ever been in a Java Web Developer situation where you had to bargain with someone? How did you feel about this? What did you do? Give an example

3. What Java Web Developer questions/answers about the other side might strengthen your position during negotiations and thus increase your chances of a successful outcome?

4. Is there anything else you can do in Java Web Developer terms of the offer?

5. Will the salary meet your needs?

6. Who can influence the Java Web Developer outcome of the talks, besides the one(s) you will negotiate with?

7. How do you call an intermission?

8. Reservation Point: What is the least you are willing to accept?

9. What is your assessment of the level of trust between you and the opposite?

10. Will you make the first offer?

11. What aspect of this negotiation was most challenging for you?

12. What does your Java Web Developer organization / chain of command / team want to have happen?

13. From your Java Web Developer perspective, what are the overarching issues?

14. What lessons can you extract from this negotiation to help Java Web Developer mentor others?

15. Is there an Java Web Developer action you can take to help develop trust (provide information, demonstrate sincerity)?

16. Closure – how do you plan on converting from divergent thinking (option Java Web Developer development) to convergent thinking (solution selection)?

17. What was the most difficult part?

18. What do you need to learn?

19. Are the offers at least as good as your best Alternative to negotiated agreement?

20. Identify your stakeholders. What are the stakeholders positions and interests?

21. Which matters most to you?

22. What if the other side plays dirty, how should you respond?

23. How much will you ask for?

24. How do you say yes, no, and maybe?

25. What should you do if you have no alternatives to agreement and the other side is big and powerful?

26. How does the salary match the research you did and your Java Web Developer range?

27. Where might your interests and the interests of the opposite coincide?

28. Do you have any Java Web Developer questions?

29. Describe the most challenging negotiation in which you were involved. What did you do? What were the Java Web Developer results for you? What were the Java Web Developer results for the other party?

30. Why are they talking to you?

31. How do you prepare for a negotiation?

32. Your BATNA?

33. What changes were you able to accommodate and why?

34. How did you resolve it?

35. What do you think they want the Java Web Developer situation to be AFTER the negotiations conclude (what is/are the opposites perceptions of longterm interest(s))?

36. Tell us about the last time you had to negotiate with someone

37. What do you need me to feel?

38. Are there any Time Bombs in your proposed offers?

39. Sequencing – How do you want to sequentially organize your negotiation?

40. What will your opening statement be the first 90 seconds?

41. Have you ever had the need to help your Java Web Developer group get on the same page to manage a conflict, ready for a transaction, or make a decision?

42. How did you prepare for it?

43. How did you present your position?

44. Do the offers satisfy the Interests youve listed?

45. Do you send the Java Web Developer information piecemeal, or wait to collect all the Java Web Developer information and send one bill?

46. Ask yourself what they other Java Web Developer sides BATNA may be. Why are they talking to you?

Delegation

1. What was the biggest mistake you have had when delegating work? The biggest Java Web Developer success?

2. Do you consider yourself a macro or Java Web Developer micro manager? How do you delegate?

3. Tell us how you go about delegating work?

4. How do you make the Java Web Developer decision to delegate work?

Toughness

1. Tell us about Java Web Developer setbacks you have faced. How did you deal with them?

2. Do you have any Java Web Developer questions about what I have talked about so far?

3. What characteristics do you think will help you to match or exceed your current high levels of functioning in the Java Web Developer future?

4. Have you any comments or Java Web Developer suggestions about the interview itself?

5. What Java Web Developer experiences do you feel will help you react positively to future challenges?

6. On many Java Web Developer occasions, managers have to make tough decisions. What was the most difficult one you have had to make?

7. What are the three greatest priorities in your Java Web Developer life?

8. What Java Web Developer suggestions would you give to senior management teams to help them better support aspiring high achievers in terms of managing and thriving on the types of demands you have been discussing?

9. What would you like to achieve in the Java Web Developer future?

10. What are some of your major accomplishments that you are most proud of?

11. Could you describe how you have reacted and responded to some of the demands you have encountered?

12. What recommendations would you give to organizations to help them aid aspiring high achievers in Java Web Developer terms of managing and thriving on the types of demands you have been discussing?

13. Can you tell me a bit about your Java Web Developer experiences as a high achiever?

14. What is the most competitive Java Web Developer situation you have experienced? How did you handle it? What was the result?

15. How have you generally felt about your Java Web Developer career challenges and how youve dealt with them?

16. Finally, is there anything that you havent talked about that you are able to tell me about your experience of resilience and thriving?

17. Did I lead you or influence your responses in any Java Web Developer way?

18. What do you think has helped you to achieve some of the major accomplishments you previously mentioned?

19. Can you tell me about some of the demands that you have had to manage during the course of your Java Web Developer career?

20. What advice or Java Web Developer suggestions would you give to aspiring high achievers to help them become more resilient and thrive on the types of situations you have been discussing?

21. Can you tell me a bit about your Java Web Developer career up to now?

22. How do you think the Java Web Developer interview went?

23. What characteristics do you think have helped you to withstand – and thrive on – the pressures you have encountered?

24. What was your major disappointment?

25. What is the foremost strength you possess (or want to possess) that proves you can achieve greatness?

26. What is your ultimate Java Web Developer goal?

27. Can you tell me about events and incidents that you feel have been particularly salient in your experience as a high achiever?

28. What do you ultimately want to achieve?

29. What has been your major work related disappointment? What happened and what did you do?

Brainteasers

1. If I roll two dice, what is the probability the sum of the amounts is nine?

2. How would you euthanize a giraffe?

3. How many ping pong balls could fit in a Boeing 747?

4. How many trees are there in NYC's Central Park?

5. What is the angle between the hour-hand and minute-hand of a clock at [time]?

6. What is your favorite Java Web Developer song? Perform it for us now.

7. How many people flew out of Cork last year?

8. If you were a pizza delivery man, how would you benefit from scissors?

9. How would you fight a bear?

10. You just got back from a 2 week vacation and have 300 emails to process in the next hour. Go.

11. How would you test a calculator?

12. Bring an Java Web Developer item with you to the interview that best represents your personality.

13. Three envelopes are presented in front of you by an

interviewer. One contains a Java Web Developer job offer, the other two contain rejection letters. You pick one of the envelopes. The interviewer then shows you the contents of one of the other envelopes, which is a rejection letter. The interviewer now gives you the opportunity to switch envelope choices. Should you switch?

14. You've got a 10 x 10 x 10 cube made up of 1 x 1 x 1 smaller cubes. The outside of the larger cube is completely painted red. On how many of the smaller cubes is there any red paint?

15. A bat and ball cost $1.10 IN TOTAL; The bat costs $1 more than the ball; How much does the ball cost?

16. I roll two fair dice, what is the probability that the sum is 9?

17. You are given 12 balls and a scale. Of the 12 balls, 11 are identical and 1 weighs slightly more. How do you find the heavier ball using the scale only three times?

18. How many boxes of breakfast cereal are sold in the US every year?

19. How many times heavier than a mouse is an elephant?

20. You are shrunk to the height of a nickel and thrown into a blender. Your mass is reduced so that your density is the same as usual. The blades start moving in 60 seconds. What do you do?

21. How many times heavier than a goldfish is a blue

whale?

22. Why is a tennis ball fuzzy?

23. With your Java Web Developer eyes closed, tell me step-by-step how to tie my shoes.

24. How many cows are in Canada?

25. How would you unload a 747 full of potatoes?

26. How many golf balls can fit in a school bus?

27. Why is there fuzz on a tennis ball?

28. How would you weigh a plane without scales?

29. How many barbers are there in Chicago?

30. Why are manhole covers round?

31. How many golf balls can you fit in a car?

32. What is the sum of numbers from 1 to 100?

33. How many gas stations are there in the U.S.?

34. How do you know if anything your Java Web Developer brain is comprehending is real - could it all just be in your Java Web Developer brain?

35. You are given 12 balls and a scale. Of the 12 balls, 11 are identical and 1 weighs EITHER slightly more or less.

How do you find the ball that is different using the scale only three times AND tell if it is heavier or lighter than the others?

36. If you could get rid of any one of the US states, which one would you get rid of and why?

37. How many times do a clock's hands overlap in a Java Web Developer day?

38. If you were an animal, which one would you want to be?

39. How many quarters (placed one on top of the other) would it take to reach the top of the Empire State Building?

40. Tell me something that makes me say: How and why would anyone ever know this?

41. Here's a mobile phone. Deconstruct it for me.

42. How many petrol stations are there in the UK?

43. If you could choose one superhero Java Web Developer power, what would it be and why?

44. How many gallons of white house paint are sold in the United States each year?

45. What are the decimal equivalents of 5/16 and 7/16?

46. Describe the color yellow to a blind person.

47. What is the sum of the numbers one to 100?

48. You have 100 balls (50 black balls and 50 white balls) and 2 buckets. How do you divide the balls into the two buckets so as to maximize the probability of selecting a black ball if 1 ball is chosen from 1 of the buckets at random?

49. Name as many uses as you can for a lemon.

50. How can you tell if the light inside your refrigerator is on or not?

51. How would you move Mount Fuji?

52. Four investment bankers need to cross a bridge at night to get to a meeting. They have only one flashlight and 17 minutes to get there. The bridge must be crossed with the flashlight and can only support two bankers at a time. The Analyst can cross in one minute, the Associate can cross in two minutes, the VP can cross in five minutes, and the MD takes 10 minutes to cross. How can they all make it to the meeting in time?

53. Sell me this pencil.

54. A car travels a distance of 60 miles at an average speed of 30 mph. How fast would the car have to travel the same 60 mile distance home to average 60 mph over the entire trip?

55. You are given a 3-gallon jug and a 5-gallon jug. How do you use them to get 4 gallons of liquid?

56. Please take this pen and sell it to me. Tell me about

its design, Java Web Developer features, benefits and values.

57. If you could be any animal, which one would you choose?

58. What colour is your Java Web Developer brain?

59. Two mothers and two daughters sit down to eat eggs for breakfast. They ate three eggs and each person at the table ate an egg. Explain how.

60. A shop owner can fit 8 large boxes or 10 medium boxes into a container for delivery. In one consignment, he distributes a total of 96 boxes. If there are more large boxes than medium boxes, how many cartons did he ship?

61. What is the angle between the hour-hand and minute-hand of a clock at 3:15?

62. How can you add eight eights to reach 1000?

63. How many gallons of paint does it take to paint the outside of the White House?

64. How would you weigh a Boeing 747 without using scales?

65. Move these three chairs from one end of the room to the other.

66. Design an evacuation plan for where we are right now.

67. How many square feet of pizza are eaten in the United States each month?

68. A windowless room has three light bulbs. You are outside the room with three switches, each controlling one of the light bulbs. If you can only enter the room one time, how can you determine which switch controls which light bulb?

69. Tell me 10 Java Web Developer ways to use a pencil other than writing.

Teamwork

1. Have you ever been a project Java Web Developer leader? Give examples of problems you experienced and how you reacted

2. Tell us about the most difficult Java Web Developer situation you have had when leading a team. What happened and what did you do? Was it successful? Emphasize the 'single' most important thing you did?

3. Tell us about the most difficult challenge you faced in trying to work cooperatively with someone who did not share the same Java Web Developer ideas? What was your role in achieving the work objective?

4. Describe your Java Web Developer leadership style and give an example of a situation when you successfully led a group

5. Describe a Java Web Developer situation in which you had to arrive at a compromise or help others to compromise. What was your role? What steps did you take? What was the end result?

6. Tell us about a time that you had to work on a Java Web Developer team that did not get along. What happened? What role did you take? What was the result?

7. When is the last time you had a disagreement with a peer? How did you resolve the Java Web Developer situation?

8. Describe a time when you struggled to build a Java

Web Developer relationship with someone important. How did you eventually overcome that?

9. Describe the Java Web Developer types of teams you've been involved with. What were your roles?

10. Talk about a time when you had to work closely with someone whose Java Web Developer personality was very different from yours.

11. Tell me about a time you needed to get Java Web Developer information from someone who wasn't very responsive. What did you do?

12. Some people work best as part of a Java Web Developer group - others prefer the role of individual contributor. How would you describe yourself? Give an example of a situation where you felt you were most effective

13. We all make Java Web Developer mistakes we wish we could take back. Tell me about a time you wish you'd handled a situation differently with a colleague.

14. Please give your best Java Web Developer example of working cooperatively as a team member to accomplish an important goal What was the goal or objective? To what extent did you interact with others on this project?

15. Tell us about the most effective Java Web Developer contribution you have made as part of a task group or special project team

16. Tell us about a work experience where you had to work closely with others. How did it go? How did you overcome any Java Web Developer difficulties?

17. Have you ever participated in a Java Web Developer task group? What was your role? How did you contribute?

18. Describe a Java Web Developer team experience you found disappointing. What would you have done to prevent this?

19. What Java Web Developer role have you typically played as a member of a team? How did you interact with other members of the team?

20. Think about the times you have been a Java Web Developer team leader. What could you have done to be more effective?

21. Give an Java Web Developer example of how you have been successful at empowering a group of people in accomplishing a task

22. Give me an Java Web Developer example of a time you faced a conflict while working on a team. How did you handle that?

23. Give an Java Web Developer example of how you worked effectively with people to accomplish an important result

24. Have you ever been in a position where you had to lead a Java Web Developer group of peers? How did you handle it?

25. Describe a Java Web Developer team experience you found rewarding

26. What is the difficult part of being a Java Web Developer member, not leader, of a team? How did you handle this?

27. When working on a Java Web Developer team project have you ever had an experience where there was strong disagreement among Java Web Developer team members? What did you do?

Decision Making

1. How do you involve your Java Web Developer manager and/or others when you make a decision?

2. What Java Web Developer kind of decisions do you make rapidly? What Java Web Developer kind takes more time? Give examples

3. Discuss an important Java Web Developer decision you have made regarding a task or project at work. What factors influenced your Java Web Developer decision?

4. Give an Java Web Developer example of a time in which you had to be relatively quick in coming to a decision

5. When you have to make a highly technical Java Web Developer decision, how do you go about doing it?

6. If you could go back in time five Java Web Developer years, what decision would you make differently? What is your best guess as to what decision you're making today you might regret five Java Web Developer years from now?

7. How have you gone about making important Java Web Developer decisions?

8. Give me an Java Web Developer example of a time when you had to keep from speaking or making a decision because you did not have enough information

9. Give an Java Web Developer example of a time when you had to be relatively quick in coming to a decision

10. What was your most difficult Java Web Developer decision in the last 6 months? What made it difficult?

11. What Java Web Developer kinds of problems have you had coordinating technical projects? How did you solve them?

12. How quickly do you make Java Web Developer decisions? Give an example

13. In a current Java Web Developer job task, what steps do you go through to ensure your decisions are correct/ effective?

14. How did you go about deciding what Java Web Developer strategy to employ when dealing with a difficult customer?

15. Give an Java Web Developer example of a time in which you had to keep from speaking or not finish a task because you did not have enough information to come to a good decision. Give an Java Web Developer example of a time when there was a decision to be made and procedures were not in place?

16. Tell us about a time when you had to defend a Java Web Developer decision you made even though other important people were opposed to your Java Web Developer decision

17. How do you go about developing I Java Web Developer information to make a decision? Give an example

18. Everyone has made some poor Java Web Developer decisions or has done something that just did not turn out right. Has this happened to you? What happened?

Scheduling

1. When all have been over-loaded, how do your people meet Java Web Developer job assignments?

2. Describe the most difficult scheduling Java Web Developer problem you have faced

3. How did you go about making Java Web Developer job assignments?

4. How did you assign priorities to Java Web Developer jobs?

Introducing Change

1. How well managed did you think a major change was?

2. What support are you getting from your Java Web Developer management team, sponsor etc?

3. What will you do to ensure that you will be able to transfer the Java Web Developer knowledge and skills obtained from your previous experiences to other colleagues?

4. Are you familiar with the content of a Java Web Developer performance management system?

5. What training did you receive?

6. What media are you using for Java Web Developer communication, and what is most effective?

7. What specific Java Web Developer actions are your managers taking to support you / your project?

8. What Java Web Developer qualities do you possess that will lead us to nominate your over other candidates?

9. Do you know what your Java Web Developer role could be in implementing a performance management system?

10. How would you define the Java Web Developer culture (the way you do things around here) within your current work environment?

11. Do people in your current work encourage each other to support the change initiatives within the organisation?

12. Have you ever had to introduce a Java Web Developer policy change to your work group? How did you do it?

13. Do you understand the purpose of implementing a Java Web Developer performance management system?

14. How do you propose to measure Java Web Developer performance or the achievement of any projects objectives?

15. Were you able to do your Java Web Developer job as well as before after a major change?

16. How have you articulated the reason for the change?

17. Have you ever met Java Web Developer resistance when implementing a new idea or policy to a work group? How did you deal with it? What happened?

18. What disruption did you feel?

19. When is the last time you had to introduce a new Java Web Developer idea or procedure to people on this job? How did you do it?

Reference

1. Who are your mentors and why?

2. How do you and X know each other?

3. If I talked to your current/past Java Web Developer manager and asked them to describe you, what would they say?

4. Can you provide 2-3 Java Web Developer references that we could shoot a quick email to that would be ok sharing their experiences of working with you?

Selecting and Developing People

1. What about this particular position and/or Java Web Developer organization most interests you?

2. Give me an Java Web Developer example of a time on the job when you disagreed with your boss or a higher-level manager. What were your options for settling the conflict?

3. Describe the project or Java Web Developer situation that best demonstrates your analytical abilities. What was your role?

4. What have you done to improve the Java Web Developer skills of your subordinates?

5. Have you ever done a research paper?

6. What Java Web Developer kinds of oral presentations have you made?

7. What, in your Java Web Developer opinion, are the key ingredients in guiding and maintaining successful relationships?

8. How often do you discuss a subordinates Java Web Developer performance with him/her?

9. Do you consider yourself a macro or Java Web Developer micro manager?

10. What Java Web Developer projects have you started on your own recently?

11. What do you do when youre having Java Web

Developer trouble solving a problem?

12. What is the most competitive work Java Web Developer situation you have experienced?

13. When was the last time you made a Java Web Developer key decision on the spur of the moment?

14. What Java Web Developer kinds of decisions are most difficult for you?

15. How do you evaluate the productivity / effectiveness of your subordinates?

16. How do you verify that you understand what someone has told you?

17. What administrative paperwork do you have?

18. How do you go about setting Java Web Developer goals with employees?

19. What have you done to further your own professional Java Web Developer development in the past 5 years?

20. Have you ever had Java Web Developer difficulty getting others to accept your ideas?

21. What was your biggest Java Web Developer success in hiring someone? What did you do?

22. Do you feel trust levels were improved as a result of your Java Web Developer actions in a certain situation?

23. How quickly do you make Java Web Developer decisions?

24. Tell us about the last time you had to negotiate with someone. What was the most difficult part?

25. How do you change an existing Java Web Developer culture to one where it is a Quality Improvement Java Web Developer culture?

26. Tell us about a Java Web Developer problem that you solved in a unique or unusual way. What was the outcome?

27. Have you ever been caught unaware by a Java Web Developer problem or obstacles that you had not foreseen?

28. How did you react when faced with constant time Java Web Developer pressure?

29. Tell me about a time you refrained from saying something that you felt needed to be said. Do you regret your Java Web Developer decision?

30. How many Java Web Developer hours a day do you put into your work?

31. How do you go about establishing rapport with a Java Web Developer customer?

32. What Java Web Developer goals did you miss?

33. What was the biggest mistake you have had when delegating work?

34. How do you determine priorities in scheduling your time?

35. Give an Java Web Developer example of when you went to the source to address a conflict. Do you feel trust levels were improved as a result?

36. What were your long-Java Web Developer range plans at your most recent employer?

37. What did you not like about being in charge?

38. What sort of work Java Web Developer hours do you normally put in?

39. Do you regret any Java Web Developer decision?

40. What Java Web Developer kind of thought process did you go through before meeting us here today?

41. Describe the most difficult Java Web Developer problem you had to solve. What was the situation and what did you do?

42. What was the most stressful Java Web Developer situation you have faced?

43. What have you done to support Java Web Developer diversity at your previous employers?

44. How do you communicate Java Web Developer goals to subordinates?

45. What were your long-Java Web Developer range plans at you most recent employer?

46. How have your Java Web Developer sales skills improved over the past three years?

47. What Java Web Developer kinds of communication situations cause you difficulty?

48. What do you do when you have multiple priorities?

49. How did you prepare?

50. What did you learn from your current Java Web Developer job or experience?

51. What new or unusual Java Web Developer ideas have you developed on your job?

52. Tell me about a time when you did something completely different from the plan and/or assignment. Why?

53. When you have Java Web Developer difficulty persuading someone to your point of view, what do you do?

54. Tell us about a recent Java Web Developer job or experience that you would describe as a real learning experience?

55. Tell me about a time when you had to sacrifice

quality to meet a deadline. How did you handle it?

56. How do you assign priorities to Java Web Developer jobs?

57. How do you learn about a Java Web Developer product or a process?

58. Describe a major change that occurred in a Java Web Developer job that you held. What did you do to adapt to this change?

59. Tell us about a time that you successfully adapted to a culturally different Java Web Developer environment. What skills made you successful?

60. How do you assemble Java Web Developer information?

61. What Java Web Developer kinds of data and technical information do you review?

62. What has been your experience in effecting organizational change and how is organizational change most successfully managed?

63. What has been your approach for bringing individuals on board who may be resistant to change?

64. Tell me how you go about delegating work?

65. Have you ever worked with a Java Web Developer colleague to solve a problem?

66. What have you done to improve the short-Java Web Developer term strength of your business unit?

67. Tell me about a Java Web Developer situation when it was important for you to pay attention to details. How did you handle it?

68. What innovative Java Web Developer procedures have you developed?

69. What have you done to develop your subordinates?

70. What do you do when your time schedule or project plan is upset by unforeseen circumstances?

71. Has a Java Web Developer problem or obstacles that you had not foreseen ever caught you unaware?

72. What do you do when priorities change quickly?

73. How would you estimate the cost of providing a new training Java Web Developer program for mid-level managers?

74. What one or two Java Web Developer things from your prior experience and/or education do you see as being the most relevant and valuable to succeed in this position?

75. How do you ensure your Java Web Developer staff is clear about which issues warrant your attention, the information you need, and delineation of authority?

76. How would you prioritize competing responsibilities, if they came in conflict?

77. How well has your Java Web Developer business/ facility/group performed?

78. What have you done to make sure that your subordinates can be productive?

79. When you have a lot of work to do, how do you get it all done?

80. What Java Web Developer kinds of problems have you had?

81. Describe the most challenging negotiation in which you were involved. What did you do?

82. What is your vision for our Quality Improvement Java Web Developer culture?

83. What is the riskiest Java Web Developer decision you have made?

84. Tell us about a time that you had to work on a Java Web Developer team that did not get along. What happened?

85. What Java Web Developer sorts of things did you do at school that was beyond expectations?

86. How do you make sure you have the Java Web Developer skills to implement the changes that will come your way and become a strategic asset?

87. What Java Web Developer solution are you the proudest of?

88. How do you coach an employee in completing a new assignment?

89. How do you manage and maintain your composure?

90. What were your annual Java Web Developer goals at your most current employer?

91. How many Java Web Developer projects do you work on at once?

92. What has been your Java Web Developer contribution to strengthen the long-term stability of your business unit?

93. What do you consider to be your professional Java Web Developer strengths?

94. What strategies would you utilize to maintain confidentiality when pressured by others?

95. If there were one Java Web Developer area youve always wanted to improve upon, what would that be?

96. What have you done to influence an Java Web Developer outcome?

97. Have you ever participated in a Java Web Developer task group?

98. What was your biggest mistake in hiring someone?

What happened? How did you deal with the Java Web Developer situation?

99. Do you often ask yourself; 'What are the high-performing policies, processes and practices that will help generate my deliverables required to support my companys Java Web Developer strategy?'

100. What was your most difficult Java Web Developer decision in the last 6 months?

101. What, if anything, did you do to mitigate negative consequences of your Java Web Developer decisions to people?

102. Give me a recent Java Web Developer example of a situation you have faced when the pressure was on. What happened?

103. What was the best Java Web Developer idea that you came up with in your career?

104. How do you handle Java Web Developer performance reviews?

105. Describe how you develop a project Java Web Developer teams goals and project plan?

106. Tell me about a time you were faced with conflicting priorities. How did you resolve the conflict?

107. What do you do when someone opposes your point of view?

108. What was your Java Web Developer role?

109. Tell me about a time you felt your Java Web Developer team was under too much pressure. What did you do about it?

110. How do you handle Java Web Developer problems with customers?

111. What, if anything, did you do to resolve Java Web Developer difficulties related to trust issues?

112. What specific Java Web Developer actions do you take to improve relationships?

113. Please describe a time when you were less than pleased with your Java Web Developer performance. How did you address this?

114. How have you helped cross-functional groups work together?

115. Have you ever had to sell an Java Web Developer idea to your co-workers or group?

116. One More Time: How Do You Motivate Java Web Developer Employees?

117. How do you get subordinates to work at their Java Web Developer peak potential?

118. Have you ever met Java Web Developer resistance when implementing a new idea or policy to a work group?

119. Have you ever had a subordinate whose work was always marginal?

120. Have you had to sell an Java Web Developer idea to your co-workers, classmates or group?

121. What are your go-to options for settling a conflict?

122. Have you ever had to persuade a Java Web Developer group to accept a proposal or idea?

123. How do you handle Java Web Developer problems with colleagues?

124. What have you done to develop your subordinates? Give an Java Web Developer example

125. How do you go about making important Java Web Developer decisions?

126. Can you tell about a time when you chose to trust someone?

127. Tell me about a time when you had to resolve a Java Web Developer difference of opinion with a coworker/ customer/supervisor. How did you feel you showed respect for that person?

128. What have you done to develop the professional Java Web Developer skills of your direct reports?

129. Have you ever had a Java Web Developer situation where you had a number of alternatives to choose from?

130. Where do you see your Java Web Developer career?

131. How do you show a person that you have understood what they have said?

132. Tell me about the most effective Java Web Developer presentation you have made. What was the topic?

133. Tell us about the most effective Java Web Developer presentation you have made. What was the topic?

134. How Do You Motivate Java Web Developer Employees?

135. Tell me about your impact on Java Web Developer sales/revenue/cost savings over the past three years. What have you done to influence it?

136. Have you ever been a Java Web Developer member of a group where two of the Java Web Developer members did not work well together?

137. How would you provide Java Web Developer feedback to me?

138. Describe a project or Java Web Developer idea that was implemented primarily because of your efforts. What was your role?

139. Have you ever been caught unaware by a Java Web Developer problem or obstacle that you had not foreseen?

140. What makes your Java Web Developer communication effective?

141. What could you have done to be more effective?

142. When have you had to produce Java Web Developer results without sufficient guidelines?

143. How do you typically confront subordinates when Java Web Developer results are unacceptable?

144. When is the last time you had to introduce a new Java Web Developer idea or procedure to people on the job?

145. How do you go about establishing rapport with a parent or community Java Web Developer member?

146. What have you done to further your Java Web Developer knowledge/understanding about diversity?

147. Describe a Java Web Developer situation that required you to do a number of things at the same time. How did you handle it?

148. How do you involve people in developing your units Java Web Developer goals?

149. What have you done or would you do to improve a Java Web Developer situation which negatively impacts results?

150. How did you ensure that another person understood?

151. When is the last time you had a disagreement with a peer?

152. What have you done to get ahead?

153. What do you do when you are faced with an obstacle to an important project?

154. When do you give positive Java Web Developer feedback to people?

155. What was the most difficult Java Web Developer decision you have had to make?

156. Have you ever had to make a major Java Web Developer decision on your own?

157. Tell us about a work experience where you had to work closely with others. How did it go?

158. Describe the Java Web Developer types of teams you have been involved with. What were your roles?

159. What Java Web Developer kinds of things really get you excited?

160. Give me an Java Web Developer example of when someone brought you a new idea that was unique or unusual. What did you do?

161. How did you go about making changes (step by step)?

162. How do you typically stay in the Java Web Developer information loop and monitor your staffs

performance?

163. What measures have you taken to make someone from a minority Java Web Developer group feel comfortable in an environment that was obviously uncomfortable with his or her presence?

164. Please tell us the number and Java Web Developer types of staff you have supervised and what differences, if any would you foresee in managing administrative vs. technical staff?

165. Tell me about your typical Java Web Developer day. How much time do you spend on the phone?

166. When you have a new Java Web Developer problem situation, how do you go about making a decision?

167. Have you ever been in a position where you had to lead a Java Web Developer group of peers?

168. When you disagree with your Java Web Developer manager, what do you do?

169. Gaining the cooperation of others can be difficult. Give a specific Java Web Developer example of when you had to do that, and what challenges you faced. What was the outcome?

170. Do you have a strategic plan?

171. How would you define a good working atmosphere?

172. Describe the most difficult working Java Web

Developer relationship you have had with an individual. What specific actions did you take to improve the Java Web Developer relationship?

173. Have you ever worked in a Java Web Developer situation where the rules and guidelines were not clear?

174. Tell us about the most difficult challenge you faced in trying to work co-operatively with someone who did not share the same Java Web Developer ideas?

175. How will you determine what issues to bring to your supervisor, which to Java Web Developer delegate to staff and which to resolve yourself?

176. Describe a time in which you were faced with Java Web Developer problems or stresses that tested your coping skills. What did you do?

177. How did you feel you showed respect for another person?

178. What Java Web Developer kinds of problems have you had coordinating technical projects?

179. What specific Java Web Developer things have you done to improve relations with parents?

180. How often do you have to rely on Java Web Developer information you have gathered from others when talking to them?

181. How well has your Java Web Developer business unit performed?

182. What was your biggest Java Web Developer success in hiring someone?

183. What do you like about being in charge?

184. How do you typically deal with conflict?

185. How do you go about setting Java Web Developer goals with subordinates?

186. What Java Web Developer sorts of things did you do at school/work that was beyond expectations?

187. Give me an Java Web Developer example of a time you had to adjust quickly to changes over which you had no control. What was the impact of the change on you?

188. What were the change/transition Java Web Developer skills that you used?

189. What do you do when your schedule is suddenly interrupted?

190. How do you go about developing Java Web Developer information to make a decision?

191. What Java Web Developer skills made you successful?

192. What was your biggest mistake in hiring someone?

193. What strategies do you use when faced with more Java Web Developer tasks than time to do them?

194. Looking back when your Java Web Developer career started to gel, what were your goals?

195. How do you go about making cold calls?

196. Is your personal Java Web Developer mission statement clear, concise, and describes what you intend to accomplish?

197. Have you ever been overloaded with work?

198. Give me an Java Web Developer example of a time you worked particularly well under a great deal of pressure. How did you handle the situation?

199. Tell me about a time when you had to help two peers settle a Java Web Developer dispute. How did you go about identifying the issues?

200. What Java Web Developer kind of decisions do you make rapidly?

201. Do you naturally Java Web Developer delegate responsibilities, or do you expect your direct reports to come to you for added responsibilities?

202. Tell us about a time when you did something completely different from the plan and/or assignment. Why?

203. How do you organize and plan for major Java Web Developer projects?

204. How do you resolve conflict?

205. Have you ever had to settle conflict between two people on the Java Web Developer job?

206. How much time do you spend on the phone?

207. Please give your best Java Web Developer example of working cooperatively as a team member to accomplish an important goal. What was the goal or objective?

208. Tell us about a recent successful experience in making a Java Web Developer speech or presentation. How did you prepare?

209. How do you present your position?

210. Describe how your position contributes to our Java Web Developer goals. What are our Java Web Developer goals?

211. What Java Web Developer kind of mentoring and training style do you have?

212. What do you do if someone at work tries to Java Web Developer pressure you to do something?

213. What could you have done to be more effective at a previous Java Web Developer job?

214. What Java Web Developer role have you typically played as a member of a team?

215. Have you ever dealt with a Java Web Developer situation where communications were poor?

216. What were your annual Java Web Developer goals at you most current employer?

217. Give me an Java Web Developer example of when you were responsible for an error or mistake. What was the outcome?

218. Have you ever been in a Java Web Developer situation where you had to bargain with someone?

219. Have you ever been a project Java Web Developer leader?

220. What has been your major work related disappointment?

221. Your supervisor left you an assignment, then left for a week. You cant reach him/her and you cant do the assignment. What would you do?

222. Can you give us an Java Web Developer example of a difficult interaction or conflict you have had with a supervisor or subordinate and how you might handle a similar situation differently (or the same) in the future?

223. When is the last time you had to introduce a new Java Web Developer idea or procedure to people on this job?

224. When was the last time that you thought outside of the box and how did you do it?

225. What is the most competitive Java Web Developer

situation you have experienced?

226. What Java Web Developer kinds of challenges did you face on your last job?

227. Describe a time where you were faced with Java Web Developer problems or stressful situations that tested your coping skills. What did you do?

228. When was the last time you were in a crisis?

229. What new Java Web Developer business opportunities did you recognize while at you last employer?

230. How do you get subordinates to produce at a high level?

231. In Java Web Developer terms of managing your staff do you expect more than you inspect or vice versa?

232. What Java Web Developer goals have you met?

233. Describe the worst on-the-Java Web Developer job crisis you had to solve. How did you manage and maintain your composure?

234. Have you ever had to introduce a Java Web Developer policy change to your work group?

235. Why were you promoted in your last Java Web Developer job?

236. What are the most challenging documents you had to create?

237. What Java Web Developer kinds of writing have you done?

238. Tell us me about an important Java Web Developer goal that you set in the past. Were you successful?

239. What were your roles?

240. What Java Web Developer company plans have you developed?

241. How do you disseminate Java Web Developer information to other people?

242. How would you define Java Web Developer success for someone in your chosen career?

243. How do you adapt to change?

244. How did you prepare for today?

245. Tell me about Java Web Developer setbacks you have faced. How did you deal with them?

246. Have you ever had to persuade a peer or Java Web Developer manager to accept an idea that you knew they would not like?

247. How would you describe the amount of structure, Java Web Developer direction, and feedback that you need to excel?

248. How have you used a question to probe for more Java Web Developer information when a person is being evasive?

249. Tell me about a time you came up with a new Java Web Developer idea. Were you able to get it approved?

250. How did you go about identifying the issues?

251. Give me an Java Web Developer example of a time you had to think quickly on your feet to extricate yourself from a difficult situation?

252. Tell me about the most difficult change you have had to make in your professional Java Web Developer career. How did you manage the change?

253. Tell me about a disagreement that you found difficult to handle. Why was it difficult?

254. Tell me about a time when you demonstrated too much initiative?

255. Which of your Java Web Developer jobs had the most rapid change?

256. Tell us about a Java Web Developer situation when it was important for you to pay attention to details. How did you handle it?

257. Trust requires personal accountability. Can you tell about a time when you chose to trust someone?

258. Describe a time when you felt that a Java Web

Developer planned change was inappropriate. What did you do?

259. Have you ever had a subordinate whose Java Web Developer performance was consistently marginal?

260. Describe a Java Web Developer situation where you, at first, resisted a change at work and later accepted it. What, specifically, changed your mind?

261. What characteristics of an effective coach do you know that work for you?

262. What Java Web Developer performance standards do you have for your unit?

263. What approach do you take in communicating with people?

Business Acumen

1. How were you rated on dependability on your last Java Web Developer job?

2. Will you be able to work this schedule?

3. Does your Java Web Developer organization create a culture that encourages learning and mentorship?

4. What aspects of the strategic-doing cycle does your Java Web Developer organization/Java Web Developer organization do well?

5. What interim systems might you need to implement?

6. How many Java Web Developer employees do you support and in what capacity?

7. In what specific Java Web Developer ways can you be a catalyst rather than a controller of change?

8. In what situations can you say yes and in which is the answer no?

9. How did you start this project?

10. Under what Java Web Developer kinds of conditions do you learn best?

11. Would you be willing to relocate if necessary?

12. Give an Java Web Developer example of a time

when you were trying to meet a deadline, you were interrupted, and did not make the deadline. How did you respond?

13. So, you can work diligently on your general propensity to trust, but some people will still let you down. Does that mean you shouldnt trust?

14. Have you ever been convicted of a felony?

15. In what Java Web Developer ways can you monitor comments and feedback?

16. How do you get people not under your authority to do work on your project?

17. How can you manage this Java Web Developer resistance?

18. What Is Your Capacity for Trust?

19. Could you share with us a recent Java Web Developer accomplishment of which you are most proud?

20. On your last expatriate assignment, what did you do to ensure that your adjustment into the new Java Web Developer environments went smoothly?

21. You are a committee Java Web Developer member and disagree with a point or decision. How will you respond?

22. What employment policies have you developed or revised?

23. What HR metrics does your current/former Java Web

Developer organization monitor?

24. Do you believe you will be remembered?

25. Have you processed payroll?

26. If I asked your previous/current co-workers about you, what would they say?

27. How did you handle the Java Web Developer situation?

28. Was there a time when you struggled to meet a deadline?

29. How Have You Responded to Change?

30. Have you ever faced a significant ethical Java Web Developer problem at work?

31. What experience have you had with tax accounting?

32. Describe a difficult time you have had dealing with an employee, Java Web Developer customer or co-worker. Why was it difficult?

33. Have you ever been over Java Web Developer budget?

34. Have you ever had to persuade a peer or superior to accept an Java Web Developer idea that you knew he/she would not like?

35. The last time that you experienced a technical Java Web Developer problem during your workday, to whom

did you go for help?

36. When you have a lot of work to do or multiple priorities, how do you get it all done?

37. Tell us about your Java Web Developer management stylepeople, teamwork, direction?

38. Tell me about a complicated Java Web Developer issue youve had to deal with. What was the Java Web Developer issue?

39. When theres a Java Web Developer decision for a new critical process, what means do you use to communicate step-by-step processes to ensure other people understand and will complete the process correctly?

40. Do You Need To Enhance Your Java Web Developer Leadership Skills?

41. What is more important to your profession, experience or continued Java Web Developer education?

42. What, if any, cost overrun issues did you have?

43. What are your child-care arrangements?

44. Can you share an Java Web Developer example of a time when you developed rapport with a customer?

45. What was the most creative thing you did in your last Java Web Developer job?

46. What have you done to help your human Java Web Developer resources department to become a strategic partner?

47. What year did you graduate from high school?

48. Do you have health-care coverage through your spouse?

49. How many Java Web Developer words per minute can you type?

50. Whats your financial signature?

51. How do you think your Java Web Developer clients/customers/guests would describe you and your work?

52. Have you worked in a Java Web Developer situation where an employee, vendor or supplier had a conflict of interest?

53. Tell me about a time when you solved one Java Web Developer problem but created others?

54. Tell me about your experience with IT systems?

55. Can you tell me about a time during your previous employment when you suggested a better Java Web Developer way to perform a process?

56. Tell me about the one person who has Java Web Developer influenced you the most during your career?

57. Have you ever solved a Java Web Developer problem that others around you could not solve?

58. Describe the workload at your current position. How do you feel about it?

59. What was the most challenging employee Java Web Developer performance issue youve had to deal with and how did you handle it?

60. What would your last Java Web Developer boss say about how you collaborate with others?

61. As our president/CEO, how would you proceed if the board of directors adopted a Java Web Developer policy or program that you felt was inconsistent with the goals and mission of our company?

62. If someone asked you for Java Web Developer assistance with a matter that is outside the parameters of your job description, what would you do?

63. What is the largest number of Java Web Developer employees you have supervised and what were their job functions?

64. How did you know you needed to make the change?

65. Have you ever managed a Java Web Developer situation where the people or units reporting to you were in different locations?

66. Tell me about a time when working in a different country you had to adapt to the Java Web Developer

culture. What adaptations did you have to make?

67. What experience do you have in multistate HR Java Web Developer management?

68. Do you trust yourself?

69. Are there any Java Web Developer types of marketing that you consider unethical?

70. What type of inventory audits have you been involved in?

71. Do you trust others?

72. What drove you, or supported you, in making the change?

73. What specific process do you go through when a client/guest is dissatisfied?

74. What criteria would you use to assess whether an employee is a rising star in your Java Web Developer organization?

75. Give an Java Web Developer example of a time when you had to quickly change project priorities. How did you do it?

76. Do you feel you are knowledgeable about current Java Web Developer industry-related legislation or trends?

77. What Java Web Developer challenges might you encounter in balancing the needs of the organization and

those of individuals?

78. How would you define guest/client satisfaction?

79. What have you done when faced with an obstacle to an important project?

80. What Java Web Developer strengths did you rely on in your last position to make you successful in your work?

81. Have you ever been involved in a department or Java Web Developer company reorganization or big change?

82. What strength could you leverage?

83. Do people ever come to you for help in solving Java Web Developer problems?

84. How do you stay current with changes in employment laws, practices and other HR issues?

85. You are angry about an unfair Java Web Developer decision. How do you react?

86. Do you tend to assume that others can be trusted until proved otherwise, or do you wait for people to prove they are trustworthy?

87. If I asked several of your co-workers about your greatest strength as a Java Web Developer team member, what would they tell me?

88. What is the HR structure in your current or most recent Java Web Developer job?

89. What are some of the Java Web Developer ways you can show respect for the knowledge, skills, and abilities of your employees or other stakeholders?

90. How well do you communicate with others?

91. How did you resolve the Java Web Developer problem?

92. How do you go about learning how our Java Web Developer organization works?

93. What does servicing the sale mean to you?

94. What will you gain?

95. How would you describe your abilities as a Java Web Developer business developer?

96. Describe your most challenging encounter with month end/year end closing. How did you resolve the Java Web Developer problem?

97. Give a specific Java Web Developer example of a decision you made that was not effective. Why do you think it was not effective, and what did you do when this realization was made?

98. Suppose you are in a Java Web Developer situation where deadlines and priorities change frequently and rapidly. How would you handle it?

99. How do you determine what amount of time is reasonable for a Java Web Developer task?

100. What would you do if faced with creating cost-cutting measures for Java Web Developer benefits premiums?

101. What do you think are the best and worst parts of working in a Java Web Developer team environment?

102. What are your major professional reading sources?

103. What Java Web Developer percentage of time did you spend on each functional area of your job?

104. We all have Java Web Developer customers or clients. –Who are your clients and how do you identify them?

105. Describe a time when you lost a Java Web Developer customer. What would you do differently?

106. What software have you had the most Java Web Developer success supporting?

107. How would people you work with describe you?

108. Describe for me a Java Web Developer decision you made that would normally have been made by your supervisor?

109. What should your Java Web Developer role be going forward?

110. Who or what drove you, or supported you, in making this Java Web Developer job change?

111. Give me an Java Web Developer example of a time when you needed to help other employees learn a new skill set. What did you do?

112. What factors Java Web Developer influenced your communication?

113. What do you do when you know you are right and your Java Web Developer boss disagrees with you?

114. In your experience, what are the essential elements of an IT disaster recovery plan?

115. What did you bring to the last position you were in?

116. Where do you see your Java Web Developer career now?

117. In what Java Web Developer types of situations can you answer yes and in which is the answer no?

118. How else can you, as a Java Web Developer leader, build trust among your constituents, whether they are employees, those above you in rank, your peers in other organizations, the media, or the public?

119. When do you think it is best to communicate in writing?

120. Describe a time you recommended a change to Java

Web Developer procedure. What did you learn from that experience?

121. How do you analyze different options to determine which is the best alternative?

122. Have you completed month end/year end closing?

123. When you have several users experiencing computer Java Web Developer problems, how do you determine which users get help first?

124. What languages do you read/speak/write fluently?

125. How can you keep Java Web Developer employees and/or stakeholders involved in the process?

126. What do you think makes a Java Web Developer team of people work well together?

127. What Java Web Developer challenges did you meet along the way?

128. What Java Web Developer difficulties did you experience adjusting to previous international assignments?

129. What was the last work-related educational Java Web Developer seminar or class you attended?

130. Do you have a personal philosophy about human Java Web Developer resources?

131. What Java Web Developer benefits experience do

you have?

132. What would be the Java Web Developer steps you would take if you were responsible for reducing staff by 10 percent?

133. In what Java Web Developer ways do you consider yourself reliable?

134. What has your current Java Web Developer company (or most recent employer) done in response to recent social changes?

135. How did you prepare yourself to make the change?

136. Describe a technical report that you had to complete. What did the report entail?

137. Describe a time when you performed a Java Web Developer task outside your perceived responsibilities. What was the Java Web Developer task?

138. Tell me about a Java Web Developer situation in which you lost it or did not do your best with a customer. What did you do about this?

139. What is your marital status?

140. What coaching or mentoring experience have you had?

141. Tell me about a time when you organized, managed and motivated others on a complex Java Web Developer task from beginning to end?

142. What did you do to adjust to a change?

143. Was the Java Web Developer success or failure of your expatriate assignments measured by your employers?

144. Whats the most valuable thing youve learned in the past year?

145. Have you ever done a cost-benefit analysis?

146. Do you belong to any professional or trade organizations that are relevant to this Java Web Developer job?

147. Java Web Developer Strategy. What was your role?

148. Tell me about your Java Web Developer policy development experiences. What employment policies have you developed or revised?

149. A new Java Web Developer policy is to be implemented organization-wide. You do not agree with this new Java Web Developer policy. How do you discuss this Java Web Developer policy with your staff?

150. Your work Java Web Developer style would complement mine?

151. What means have you used to keep from making Java Web Developer mistakes?

152. An employee tells you about a sexual harassment

allegation but then tells you he or she doesnt want to do anything about it; he/she just thought you should know. How do you respond?

153. When making a Java Web Developer decision to terminate employment of an employee, do you find it easy because of the companys needs or difficult because of the employees needs?

154. What metrics did you use to measure ongoing project status?

155. How can you sustain energy and commitment to a change over time?

156. Do You Have The Java Web Developer Business Acumen For Success?

157. Give me an Java Web Developer example of a time when you had to deal with a difficult co-worker. How did you handle the situation?

158. Have you ever worked in a virtual Java Web Developer team?

159. How have you reacted when you found yourself stalled in an inefficient process?

160. Have you ever been engaged in Java Web Developer team sales?

161. What do you do when someone else is late and preventing you from accomplishing your Java Web Developer tasks?

162. What small successes can you celebrate?

163. What do you think is the Java Web Developer role of the president/CEO in strategic planning for the organization?

164. What type of Java Web Developer projects have you managed in the past?

165. How can you walk the talk during a change initiative?

166. Have you ever given a Java Web Developer presentation to a group?

167. What are some of the specific Java Web Developer ways you demonstrate that you do what you say?

168. What type of training/Java Web Developer education did you receive in the military?

169. Give an Java Web Developer example of how you carefully considered your audience prior to communicating with them. What factors influenced your communication?

170. Have you had an occasion when a prior strength actually turned out to be a Java Web Developer weakness in another setting?

171. How many expatriate assignments have you completed?

172. What does Java Web Developer customer mean to you?

173. Describe a time when you had to deal with a difficult Java Web Developer boss, co-worker or customer. How did you handle the situation?

174. What are your Java Web Developer career path interests?

175. Java Web Developer careers grow and develop just like people do. Where do you see your Java Web Developer career now?

176. In what Java Web Developer ways do you consider yourself unreliable?

177. If you are hired for this position and are still with (name of Java Web Developer company/organization) five years from now, how do you think the organization will be different?

178. What Java Web Developer area of your last job was most challenging for you?

179. Have you had a non-productive Java Web Developer team member on your project Java Web Developer team?

180. How do you go about deciding what Java Web Developer strategy to employ when dealing with a difficult customer?

181. What clubs or social organizations do you belong to?

182. You have a critical Java Web Developer decision to make for your department, and all alternatives will likely be unpopular with your staff. What input do you gather

before deciding?

183. What Java Web Developer types of behaviors do you find most annoying or frustrating in a client/customer?

184. What Java Web Developer kind of experience do you have with training employees and managers?

185. What Java Web Developer input do you gather before deciding?

186. What adaptations did you have to make?

187. How do you discuss a Java Web Developer policy with your staff?

188. What experience do you have with financial planning and analysis?

189. How have you approached solving a Java Web Developer problem that initially seemed insurmountable?

190. Describe for me a time when you have come across questionable accounting practices. How did you handle the Java Web Developer situation?

191. What recruiting experience do you have?

192. Tell me about a time when you had a work Java Web Developer problem and didnt know what to do?

193. Describe a time when you took a new Java Web

Developer job that required a much different set of skills from what you had. How did you go about acquiring the needed skills?

194. What do you think of your last Java Web Developer boss?

195. Whats Your Financial Java Web Developer Style?

196. What is your own philosophy of Java Web Developer management?

197. Describe some recent Java Web Developer projects you were involved in to improve accountings efficiency / effectiveness. What did you do?

198. What do you believe is your most honed Java Web Developer skill?

199. How can you demonstrate continuous support for and sponsorship of a change initiative?

200. What brands of hardware do you feel most comfortable dealing with?

201. What approach and philosophy did you follow in working with boards?

202. Describe a Java Web Developer situation where you have had to work in a multicultural environment and the challenges you had. How did you approach the Java Web Developer situation and what was the outcome?

203. What characteristics do you feel are necessary for

Java Web Developer success as a technical support worker?

204. What mechanisms can you use to solicit employee and/or stakeholder concerns?

205. Does your Java Web Developer organization have a formal process for career development?

206. Tell me about a time when big changes took place in your Java Web Developer job. What did you do to adjust to the change?

207. What are your Java Web Developer organization s Core Values and Competencies?

208. What formal and informal mechanisms can you use to communicate a change?

209. Can you work within the confines of a x-foot aisle?

210. What methods do you use to make Java Web Developer decisions?

211. What Java Web Developer things get in the way of successful strategic doing in your organization/ organization?

212. What would you have done differently?

213. How would your co-workers describe your work Java Web Developer style/habits?

214. We are seeking Java Web Developer employees who focus on detail. What means have you used to keep from

making mistakes?

215. What control measures/Java Web Developer techniques would you put in place to overcome risks?

216. How did you go about acquiring the needed Java Web Developer skills?

217. What Java Web Developer actions can you take to ensure that your interJava Web Developer actions with employees and/or stakeholders are and will remain unguarded?

218. What Java Web Developer kinds of investigations have you had to complete?

219. You're new to an Java Web Developer organization. How do you go about learning how that Java Web Developer organization works?

220. Are you able to perform the essential functions of the Java Web Developer job?

221. What support, either administrative or technical Java Web Developer assistance, did you receive in your previous positions?

222. When was the date of your last physical exam?

223. How would you start this project?

224. Suppose your supervisor asked you to get Java Web Developer information for him or her that you knew was confidential and he/she should not have access to. What

would you do?

225. What potential Java Web Developer resistance points might you encounter?

226. What is your native language?

227. Have you worked under time constraints before?

228. In what areas would you like to develop further?

229. What do you look for when considering whether another person is trustworthy?

230. What was one of the toughest Java Web Developer problems you ever solved?

231. Describe for me a time when you have come across questionable Java Web Developer business practices. How did you handle the situation?

232. People react differently when Java Web Developer job demands are constantly changing. How do you react to this?

233. Throughout your Java Web Developer career have you learned more about your profession through coursework or through on the job experience?

234. Have you ever had to champion an unpopular change?

235. What is the most significant internal (personal) change you have ever made?

236. What was the last big project you worked on?

237. Tell me about a time when you thought someone wasnt listening to you. What did you do?

238. In what Java Web Developer ways or in what situations do you have the least capacity for trust?

239. When it comes to giving Java Web Developer information to employees that can be done either way, do you prefer to write an email/memo or talk to the employee?

240. What compensation experience do you have?

241. Tell me about your experience working with a board of directors. What approach and philosophy did you follow in working with boards?

242. Have you ever worked in a union Java Web Developer environment?

243. What are the Core Java Web Developer Leadership Competencies needed for your organization?

244. Tell me about a work nightmare you were involved in. How did you approach the Java Web Developer situation and what was the outcome?

245. What do you do to develop Java Web Developer employees you manage?

246. Solutions: what specific Java Web Developer actions will you take to address specific priorities?

247. What vendor Java Web Developer relationships were you responsible for managing?

248. What was the best training Java Web Developer program in which you have participated?

Responsibility

1. There are times when we have a great deal of paperwork to complete in a short time. How do you do to ensure your Java Web Developer accuracy?

2. What are two or three Java Web Developer examples of tasks that you do not particularly enjoy doing? Tell us how you remain motivated to complete those tasks.

3. Have you Java Web Developer planned any conferences, workshops or retreats? What steps did you take to plan the event?

4. What can you tell us about yourself that you feel is unique and makes you the best Java Web Developer candidate for this position?

5. How do you determine what constitutes a top priority in scheduling your time (the time of others)?

6. We often have to push ourselves harder to reach a Java Web Developer target. Give us a specific example of when you had to give yourself that extra push.

7. Tell us about a demanding Java Web Developer situation in which you managed to remain calm and composed. What did you do and what was the outcome?

8. Tell us about a time when you put in some extra Java Web Developer effort to help move a particular project forward. How did you do it and what happened?

9. Tell us about a time when you achieved Java Web Developer success through your willingness to react quickly.

10. Tell us about a time when you disagreed with a Java Web Developer procedure or policy instituted by management. What was your reaction and how did you implement the Java Web Developer procedure or policy?

11. If I call your Java Web Developer references, what will they say about you?

12. What has been your greatest Java Web Developer success, personally or professionally?

13. Give an Java Web Developer example of a time you noticed a process or task that was not being done correctly. How did you discover or come to notice it, and what did you do?

14. Describe a time when you had to make a difficult Java Web Developer decision on the job. What facts did you consider? How long did it take you to make a Java Web Developer decision?

15. Do you have a Java Web Developer system for organizing your own work area? Tell us how that Java Web Developer system helped you on the job.

16. Java Web Developer Jobs differ in the extent to which people work independently or as part of a team. Tell us about a time when you worked independently.

17. What Java Web Developer kinds of measures have you taken to make sure all of the small details of a project

or assignment were done? Please give a specific example.

18. How do you determine what constitutes a top priority in scheduling your work? Give a specific Java Web Developer example.

19. What Java Web Developer strengths do you have that we haven't talked about?

20. It is often easy to blur the Java Web Developer distinction between confidential information and public knowledge. Have you ever been faced with this dilemma? What did you do?

21. Tell us about a time when the Java Web Developer details of something you were doing were especially important. How did you attend to them?

22. Tell us about a time when you had to review detailed reports or documents to identify a Java Web Developer problem. How did you go about it? What did you do when you discovered a Java Web Developer problem?

Client-Facing Skills

1. Tell me about a time when you made sure a Java Web Developer customer was pleased with your service.

2. Describe a time when it was especially important to make a good Java Web Developer impression on a client. How did you go about doing so?

3. How do you go about prioritizing your Java Web Developer customers' needs?

4. Describe a time when you had to interact with a difficult client. What was the Java Web Developer situation, and how did you handle it?

5. Give me an Java Web Developer example of a time when you did not meet a client's expectation. What happened, and how did you attempt to rectify the situation?

Planning and Organization

1. How do you schedule your time? Set priorities? How do you handle doing twenty Java Web Developer things at once?

2. What do you do when your time schedule or project plan is upset by unforeseen circumstances? Give an Java Web Developer example

3. Describe how you develop a project team's Java Web Developer goals and project plan?

4. What have you done in order to be effective with your Java Web Developer organization and planning?

5. Tell us about a time when you organized or Java Web Developer planned an event that was very successful

Motivating Others

1. How do you get subordinates to produce at a high level? Give an Java Web Developer example

2. How do you get subordinates to work at their Java Web Developer peak potential? Give an example

3. How do you manage cross-functional Java Web Developer teams?

4. How do you deal with people whose work exceeds your expectations?

5. Have you ever had a subordinate whose work was always marginal? How did you deal with that person? What happened?

Customer Orientation

1. How do you handle Java Web Developer problems with customers? Give an example

2. How do you go about establishing rapport with a Java Web Developer customer? What have you done to gain their confidence? Give an example

3. What have you done to improve Java Web Developer relations with your customers?

Unflappability

1. There are times when we all have to deal with deadlines and it can be stressful. Tell us about a time when you felt pressured at work and how you coped with it.

2. Describe Java Web Developer suggestions you have made to improve work procedures. How did it turn out?

3. Give us an Java Web Developer example of when you made a presentation to an uninterested or hostile audience. How did it turn out?

4. Tell us about a time when you put in some extra Java Web Developer effort to help move a project forward. How did you do that? What happened?

5. We have to find Java Web Developer ways to tolerate and work with difficult people. Tell us about a time when you have done this.

6. Many times, a Java Web Developer job requires you to quickly shift your attention from one task to the next. Tell us about a time at work when you had to change focus onto another task. What was the outcome?

7. On occasion, we experience conflict with our superiors. Describe such a Java Web Developer situation and tell us how you handled the conflict. What was the outcome?

8. Tell us about a time when you received accurate, negative Java Web Developer feedback by a co-worker, boss, or customer. How did you handle the evaluation?

How did it affect your work?

9. Give us an Java Web Developer example of a demanding situation when you were able to maintain your composure while others got upset.

10. Give us an Java Web Developer example of when you felt overly sensitive to feedback or criticism. How did you handle your feelings?

Extracurricular

1. What did you do in Java Web Developer college aside from going to school?

2. What do you do for Java Web Developer fun and what hobbies do you partake in when you are not at work?

3. What's next on your Java Web Developer bucket list and why?

4. Have you ever played a Java Web Developer team sport?

5. Identify a project or Java Web Developer task that you would be the most proud of and would consider your most significant accomplishment in your career to date and describe the circumstances. How you got involved, your contributions and participation along with your reasoning on why this is the one you picked?

6. Based on all the facets of our Java Web Developer company (big data, unconscious bias, diversity, analytics, mobile apps, etc) what relevant work have you done OUTSIDE OF WORK?

7. Have you ever created any side-Java Web Developer projects or organized any community events?

8. What are the three most interesting just-for-Java Web Developer fun projects you've built?

Setting Goals

1. What Java Web Developer goals did you miss? Why did you miss them?

2. How do you involve people in developing your unit's Java Web Developer goals? Give an example

3. What were your long-Java Web Developer range plans at your most recent employer? What was your role in developing them?

4. How do you communicate Java Web Developer goals to subordinates? Give an example

5. What Java Web Developer company plans have you developed? Which ones have you reached? How did you reach them? Which have you missed? Why did you miss them?

6. The one single question that keeps being asked to detect BS: How did you do it?

7. What Java Web Developer goals have you met? What did you do to meet them?

8. Did you have a strategic plan? How was it developed? How did you communicate it to the rest of your Java Web Developer staff?

9. What were your annual Java Web Developer goals at your most current employer? How did you develop these Java Web Developer goals?

10. What is something that you accomplished in the last 2 Java Web Developer years that required a high amount

of grit?

Flexibility

1. What does being a flexible communicator give to you ?

2. Why do you need to be a good communicator?

3. Which NLP preference sounds most like you?

4. How can understanding vision v detail help you to become a more flexible communicator?

5. What Java Web Developer problems/weak areas do your interventions address?

6. How often do you think about good Java Web Developer things related to your job when youre busy doing something else?

7. All in all, how satisfied are you with your Java Web Developer job?

8. Why you need to be a good communicator?

9. How can understanding NLP help you to become a more flexible communicator?

10. What do other people need from you?

11. Which DISC Java Web Developer personality is the toughest for you to communicate with?

12. How have you adjusted your Java Web Developer style when it was not meeting the objectives and/or

people were not responding correctly?

13. What is flexibility and why is it important to maintain flexibility and continue to stretch throughout your whole entire Java Web Developer life?

14. What do you do when you are faced with an obstacle to an important project? Give an Java Web Developer example

15. What would be a win/win for you and me both?

16. What Java Web Developer questions should you be asking?

17. When you have Java Web Developer difficulty persuading someone to your point of view, what do you do? Give an example

18. Have you ever had a subordinate whose Java Web Developer performance was consistently marginal? What did you do?

19. Getting better at which Java Web Developer skill would make the biggest difference to improving your flexibility as a communicator?

20. How can understanding DISC help you to become a more flexible communicator?

21. How can you increase your own flexibility?

Leadership

1. Give an Java Web Developer example of a time in which you felt you were able to build motivation in your co-workers or subordinates at work

2. Have you ever been a Java Web Developer member of a group where two of the Java Web Developer members did not work well together? What did you do to get them to do so?

3. Have you ever had Java Web Developer difficulty getting others to accept your ideas? What was your approach? Did it work?

4. What is the toughest Java Web Developer group that you have had to get cooperation from? Describe how you handled it. What was the outcome?

5. What is the toughest Java Web Developer group that you have had to get cooperation from?

6. Give an Java Web Developer example of your ability to build motivation in your co-workers, classmates, and even if on a volunteer committee

Evaluating Alternatives

1. What are some of the major Java Web Developer decisions you have made over the past (6, 12, 18) months?

2. What alternatives did you develop?

3. How did you review the Java Web Developer information? What process did you follow to reach a conclusion?

4. How did you assemble the Java Web Developer information?

5. Have you ever had a Java Web Developer situation where you had a number of alternatives to choose from? How did you go about choosing one?

6. What Java Web Developer kinds of decisions are most difficult for you? Describe one?

Business Systems Thinking

1. What do you think about Java Web Developer business system thinking and ethical dilemmas?

2. Where, geographically, does our market have strong holds?

3. Do you consider ethics an important aspect of doing Java Web Developer business?

4. Are you aware, in general Java Web Developer terms, of the functions and responsibilities of this role?

5. Do you feel that ones moral Java Web Developer standards should equal or exceed their companys code of ethics?

6. Does our companys image match with your brands and products?

7. To what extent do you agree that ethical Java Web Developer standards begins at the highest levels of the firm?

8. Would you trust a firm whos ethical Java Web Developer standards were considered to be/have been suspect?

9. Do you agree that creativity can be motivated through incentives?

10. Do you agree that a salespersons fear of change heightens ones readiness when faced with different Java Web Developer performance procedures?

11. Do you agree that having the accessibility of creative, Java Web Developer communication tools increases the possibility of creative thinking?

12. Describe how your position contributes to your organization's/unit's Java Web Developer goals. What are the unit's Java Web Developer goals/mission?

13. Do you agree that the setting of the Java Web Developer organization impacts how innovative its salespersons are in their selling approaches?

14. What Do You Need From Me?

15. Whom do you serve?

16. Tell us about a politically complex work Java Web Developer situation in which you worked

17. Is Six Sigma a Good Fit for our Java Web Developer Business?

18. Are you aware of the Java Web Developer relationship of sales engineeeers in new product development and customer sales?

19. Are you aware, in general Java Web Developer terms, of the functions and responsibilities of a sales engineer?

20. What would be the affect on our Java Web Developer customers lives if you did not exist to do your work?

21. Who Is Your Java Web Developer Leadership?

22. What is our Java Web Developer organization about and how does PM/QI/Accreditation support that?

23. Would you agree that Offensive Marketing would be valuable for having created superior and recognized Java Web Developer customer value as well as having achieved above-average profits?

24. Do you agree that Java Web Developer companies that have a more flexible atmosphere are more prone to creative thinking?

25. Would you feel that one of the most important assets of businesses would be its new Java Web Developer product development?

26. Do you believe our Java Web Developer product is one that will last or is the market a fad?

27. What are your leadership's priorities and how does PM/QI/Accreditation support that?

28. Do you agree that Effective Marketing, through brand equity, has played an important Java Web Developer role in establishing distinct advantages towards our firms marketing perceived value from its marketplace?

29. Are you aware, in general Java Web Developer terms, of the functions and responsibilities of marketing research firms?

30. Do you agree that creativity can be taught?

31. Are you aware of the Java Web Developer relationship of sales engineers in new product development and customer sales?

32. Do you agree that the more authority a salespersons possesses, the higher their probability of coming up with innovative Java Web Developer ideas?

33. To what extent are you knowledgeable of the new 6th P in the marketing mix, Poise?

34. Is your current Java Web Developer company properly structured for the future of market opportunities and challenges?

35. Why are you really winning and losing deals?

36. To what extent are you aware of the Java Web Developer company-wide applications of Poise?

37. Do you agree that the more extensive a salespersons experience, the less relevant adaptability becomes to that person?

38. Do you agree that the higher a Java Web Developer salesperson perceives the value of adaptability, the higher the likely increase in Java Web Developer sales revenue?

39. Who is our Java Web Developer target market?

Integrity

1. Give Java Web Developer examples of how you have acted with integrity in your job/work relationship

2. If you can, tell about a time when your trustworthiness was challenged. How did you react/respond?

3. Tell us about a specific time when you had to handle a tough Java Web Developer problem which challenged fairness or ethnical issues

4. Describe a time when you were asked to keep Java Web Developer information confidential

5. Trust requires personal accountability. Can you tell about a time when you chose to trust someone? What was the Java Web Developer outcome?

6. On occasion we are confronted by dishonesty in the workplace. Tell about such an occurrence and how you handled it

Time Management Skills

1. Tell me about a time you had to be very strategic in order to meet all your top priorities.

2. Give me an Java Web Developer example of a time you managed numerous responsibilities. How did you handle that?

3. Tell me about a time you set a Java Web Developer goal for yourself. How did you go about ensuring that you would meet your objective?

4. Of your current assignments, which do you consider to have required the greatest amount of Java Web Developer effort with regard to planning/organization? How have you accomplished this assignment? How would you asses your effectiveness?

5. Describe a long-Java Web Developer term project that you managed. How did you keep everything moving along in a timely manner?

6. How do you determine priorities in scheduling your time? Give an Java Web Developer example

7. Describe a Java Web Developer situation that required you to do a number of things at the same time. How did you handle it? What was the result?

8. How do you typically plan your Java Web Developer day to manage your time effectively?

9. Sometimes it's just not possible to get everything on your to-do list done. Tell me about a time your responsibilities got a little overwhelming. What did you

do?

Detail-Oriented

1. Have the Java Web Developer jobs you held in the past required little attention, moderate attention, or a great deal of attention to detail? Give me an example of a situation that illustrates this requirement

2. Describe a Java Web Developer situation where you had the option to leave the details to others or you could take care of them yourself

3. Do you prefer to work with the 'big Java Web Developer picture' or the 'details' of a situation? Give me an example of an experience that illustrates your preference?

4. Tell us about a difficult experience you had in working with Java Web Developer details

5. Tell us about a Java Web Developer situation where attention to detail was either important or unimportant in accomplishing an assigned task

Most Common

1. I'm not sure you're the perfect fit. Why do you think you'd be a great Java Web Developer candidate?

2. How would you handle a Java Web Developer team situation where Nina wants to dive right in, Joe is telecommuting, and Todd wants to gut the project?

3. Why do you want to work for _____?

4. What are you looking to gain out of associating with our brokerage?

5. How do you prepare for Java Web Developer meetings and facilitate Java Web Developer meetings? What do you make sure to do during a meeting?

6. What do you need in your physical Java Web Developer workspace to be successful in your job?

7. When do you feel that it is justified for you to go against accepted Java Web Developer principles or policy?

8. How would you evaluate your present firm?

9. Briefly walk me through your Java Web Developer background and experience as it relates to our opening.

10. Would you have a Java Web Developer problem cleaning the toilets?

11. Do you prefer Java Web Developer staff or line work? Why?

12. A snail is at the bottom of a 30-foot well. Each Java Web Developer day he climbs up three feet, but at night he slips back two feet. How many Java Web Developer days will it take him to climb out of the well?

13. How do you use Java Web Developer technology throughout the day, in your job and for pleasure?

14. How much are you looking for?

15. How well do you handle rejection?

16. Out of all the other Java Web Developer candidates, why should we hire you?

17. What did you earn in your last Java Web Developer job? What level of salary are you looking for now?

18. What are you most proud of?

19. Where do you see yourself in five Java Web Developer years? Ten Java Web Developer years?

20. Tell me about a time when you had to deal with an irate Java Web Developer customer. How did you handle the situation?

21. Give me Java Web Developer proof of your persuasiveness.

22. Do You Have Interviews With Other Java Web Developer Companies?

23. How long would it take you to make a meaningful Java Web Developer contribution to our firm?

24. Why Do You Want To Work For Our Java Web Developer Company?

25. What do you think of our Java Web Developer competitors?

26. What does "working remotely" actually look like for you?

27. When I speak to your last [or present] Java Web Developer boss, what is he or she going to say about you?

28. Where else have you applied to?

29. What makes you uncomfortable?

30. What are your biggest Java Web Developer strengths?

31. When have you gone beyond the Java Web Developer limits of your authority in making a decision?

32. Give an Java Web Developer example of a situation where you reluctantly delegated to a colleague. How did you feel about it?

33. Why Do You Want To Work At [Java Web Developer Company Name]?

34. What did you like, dislike about your last Java Web Developer job?

35. Tell me about an important Java Web Developer decision you had to make... how did you go about deciding?

36. Where do you see yourself in 3 , 5, 10 Java Web Developer years time?

37. What were your Java Web Developer bosses' strengths / weaknesses?

38. What are your computing Java Web Developer skills like?

39. Give an Java Web Developer example of a project or task that you felt compelled to complete on your own. What stopped you from delegating?

40. Have you ever been asked to do something illegal, immoral or against your Java Web Developer principles? What did you do?

41. What are some of your Java Web Developer leadership experiences?

42. What important Java Web Developer trends do you see in our industry?

43. Why Are You Leaving Your Current Java Web Developer Job?

44. If you made it all the Java Web Developer way to the end of this guide, bravo! What did we miss here in our

best interview questions guide? Do you have a favorite interview question you like to ask? What is it?

45. What is the biggest challenge that you have faced in your Java Web Developer career. How did you overcome it?

46. Who's your Java Web Developer mentor?

47. Have you ever been in a Java Web Developer situation where you disagreed with your manager? How did you resolve the disagreement?

48. What are your aspirations beyond this Java Web Developer job?

49. How do you take Java Web Developer direction?

50. How do you ensure that you maintain good working Java Web Developer relationships with your senior colleagues?

51. How would your last Java Web Developer boss or your coworkers describe you?

52. What special qualifications and Java Web Developer experiences do you have?

53. Are you a good Java Web Developer manager? Give an example. Why do you feel you have top Java Web Developer managerial potential?

54. Have you ever ran an entrepreneurial Java Web Developer business, even something as simple as selling collectible cards in high school?

55. How do you utilize the Internet, video tours, and social media to sell property or homes?

56. What would your current Java Web Developer manager say are your strengths?

57. In your current or last position, what Java Web Developer features did you like the most? Least?

58. Why haven't you found a new position before now?

59. Tell us about a Java Web Developer situation where you made a decision that involuntarily impacted negatively on others. How did you make that decision and how did you handle its consequences?

60. Do you have any Java Web Developer questions or concerns about your ability to do the job?

61. What do you look for in a Java Web Developer job?

62. Why do you think you would like working for us?

63. Why Did You Switch Java Web Developer Career Paths?

64. What are your hobbies?

65. What has been your greatest achievement?

66. What are your Java Web Developer future goals?

67. What place does empathy play in your work? Give an Java Web Developer example where you needed to show empathy.

68. What is the Java Web Developer decision that you have put off the longest? Why?

69. Why would you want a position like this?

70. When did you depart from the Java Web Developer party line to accomplish your goal?

71. What is a Java Web Developer quarter of a half?

72. Tell me how you handled a difficult Java Web Developer situation.

73. Do You Have Any Java Web Developer Questions For Us?

74. Why do you think Java Web Developer graduates in .. [your degree subject] .. would be good at .. [job role you have applied for] .. ?

75. I checked out your last company's social media accounts to see what your marketing department has been up to. What did you think of their current campaign?

76. What motivates you to deliver your greatest Java Web Developer effort?

77. What motivates you?

78. How did you reach the Java Web Developer decision that you wanted to change your job?

79. How would you explain a 10% departmental salary cut and still retain Java Web Developer loyalty?

80. Why should I hire you vs the next person (or robot) to walk through the door?

81. What's your availability?

82. What Are You Looking For In This Java Web Developer Job?

83. (If you have had interviews) Why do you think you haven't been offered a Java Web Developer job yet?

84. How do you schedule your Java Web Developer day?

85. How do you handle Java Web Developer pressure?

86. Have you ever had to work with a person you didn't get along with? How did you handle the Java Web Developer problem?

87. How do you build Java Web Developer relationships with other members of your team?

88. Do you have an established farm Java Web Developer area? Are you planning on staying there?

89. What would you do for us? What can you do for us

that someone else can't?

90. What Would Be Something That Would Make our Java Web Developer Company Hesitate and Not Hire You?

91. You have not done this sort of Java Web Developer job before. How will you succeed?

92. Describe a typical work week for you.

93. What has been the biggest disappointment in your Java Web Developer life?

94. Give us an Java Web Developer example of when you have worked to an unreasonable deadline or been faced with a huge challenge.

95. What Java Web Developer questions do you have for us?

96. Are you a Java Web Developer leader?

97. Have you ever had a conflict with a Java Web Developer boss or professor? How was it resolved?

98. Do you feel you might be better off in a different size Java Web Developer company? Different type Java Web Developer company?

99. If we hire you, how will you help grow your Java Web Developer business (through our agency)?

100. How would you handle Java Web Developer lack of face-to-face contact when you work remotely?

101. Describe a project where you needed to involve Java Web Developer input from other departments. How did you identify that need and how did you ensure buy-in from the appropriate leaders and managers?

102. Where do you see yourself in 5 Java Web Developer years?

103. What's the Java Web Developer job you want two Java Web Developer jobs from now, and how does this role help you get there?

104. Have you ever had to learn a Java Web Developer skill and then apply it immediately?

105. Give us an Java Web Developer example of a situation where you faced conflict or difficult communication problems

106. Wow, (insert Java Web Developer company name from their resume) is an impressive Java Web Developer company, but I've heard their culture is a bit (insert adjective that you know of Java Web Developer company culture). How did you find you fit into that culture?

107. What would your current Java Web Developer manager say are your weaknesses?

108. What two or three Java Web Developer things would be most important to you in your ideal job, and why?

109. Tell me about your Java Web Developer skills in (insert crucial skill for the role). How many years

experience do you have in it and how would you rate yourself on a 1-10 scale, with 10 being an expert?

110. What do you see as the most difficult Java Web Developer task in being a manager?

111. What interests you about this Java Web Developer job?

112. Tell me about a time when you Java Web Developer planned and arranged a large project or event? What steps did you take?

113. If you had a Java Web Developer problem when the rest of your remote team was offline, how would you go about solving it?

114. How did you end up in the administrative field?

115. What was your biggest mistake as a new Java Web Developer agent? Have you overcome it? How?

116. What is your Java Web Developer management style?

117. How do you go about solving Java Web Developer problems?

118. Have you ever been on a Java Web Developer team where someone was not pulling their own weight? How did you handle it?

119. What did you like best and least in your last

position?

120. What is the worst Java Web Developer communication situation that you have experienced?

121. How do you resolve conflict on a project Java Web Developer team?

122. What big Java Web Developer decision did you make recently. How did you go about it?

123. What is your most valuable asset when it comes to remote work?

124. What interests do you have outside work?

125. How would you weigh an airplane, like a Boeing 747, without a scale?

126. What is your biggest Java Web Developer weakness as a manager?

127. Why are you leaving your current brokerage?

128. Tell me about a time when you worked as part of a Java Web Developer team? How did you handle it?

129. What are three Java Web Developer things your former manager would like you to improve on?

130. How do you prepare for an important meeting?

131. Why do you like to manage people?

132. What are you looking for in your next Java Web Developer job? What is important to you?

133. What do you like to do outside of work?

134. Do you generally speak to people before they speak to you?

135. What Do You Do For Java Web Developer Fun?

136. When is that last time that you had an Java Web Developer argument with a colleague?

137. Are you creative?

138. Tell me about a time you made a mistake.

139. If you know your Java Web Developer boss is 100% wrong about something, how would you handle this?

140. Do you have any Java Web Developer questions about the job or the company?

141. Why do you think this Java Web Developer industry would sustain your interest in the long haul?

142. What would you look to accomplish in the first 30 days/60 days/90 days on the Java Web Developer job?

143. What are your biggest accomplishments?

144. What is your Java Web Developer leadership style?

145. Do you like working in a Java Web Developer team environment or do you prefer working alone?

146. Describe your approach to Java Web Developer problem-solving?

147. Describe one of your current or recently completed Java Web Developer projects, setting out the risks involved. How did you make decisions? How do you know that you made the correct decisions?

148. Do you work best independently or as part of a Java Web Developer team?

149. How have you helped increase Java Web Developer sales? Profits?

150. How would your worst enemy describe you?

151. How do you handle criticism?

152. What blogs and Java Web Developer resources do you follow online to keep up with the industry?

153. What sort of salary are you looking for?

154. What Java Web Developer challenges are you looking for in this position?

155. How do you balance your work Java Web Developer

life and the rest of your Java Web Developer life?

156. What Are Your Professional Java Web Developer Strengths?

157. Describe a Java Web Developer situation where you had to explain something complex to a colleague or a client. Which problems did you encounter and how did you deal with them?

158. What are your pet peeves?

159. What Java Web Developer risks do you see in moving to this new post?

160. What gets you out of bed in the morning?

161. Which constraints are imposed on you in your current Java Web Developer job and how do you deal with these?

162. What other careers have you considered/applied for?

163. Under what Java Web Developer conditions do you work best and worst?

164. Did you enjoy Java Web Developer university?

165. Describe your ideal Java Web Developer job?

166. Tell us about an unpopular Java Web Developer decision that you made recently? What thought-

process did you follow before making it? How did your colleagues/clients react and how did you deal with their reaction?

167. What new Java Web Developer skills are you looking to develop this year?

168. How many transaction Java Web Developer sides did you close this year?

169. Did you ever fire anyone? If so, what were the Java Web Developer reasons and how did you handle it?

170. How would you deconstruct a mobile phone? Explain it to me like I had never seen it before.

171. Describe yourself.

172. Tell me about a time you disagreed with a Java Web Developer decision. What did you do?

173. Why do you want to work as a real Java Web Developer estate agent?

174. Give us an Java Web Developer example of a situation where you knew that a project or task would place you under great pressure. How did you plan your approach and remain motivated?

175. What would you say are your weak Java Web Developer points?

176. What was it about this Java Web Developer job description that caught your eye?

177. Would you describe a Java Web Developer situation in which your work was criticized?

178. In your current or last position, what are or were your five most significant accomplishments?

179. What do you expect to be doing in five Java Web Developer years' time?

180. Tell me about an Java Web Developer accomplishment you are most proud of.

181. When have you had to lie to achieve your aims? Why did you do so? How do you feel you could have achieved the same aim in a different Java Web Developer way?

182. What do you look for when you hire people?

183. When is the last time that you were upset with yourself?

184. How do you organize Java Web Developer files, links, and tabs on your computer?

185. What can we expect from you in your first three months?

186. What drives you to achieve your objectives?

187. Why did you choose your Java Web Developer degree subject?

188. When was the last time you were angry and what

happened?

189. If we gave you a new project to manage, how would you decide how to approach it?

190. Who are our Java Web Developer competitors?

191. What do you think you will be doing in this Java Web Developer role?

192. If a work teammate were to come in tomorrow morning and tell you he or she is quitting tomorrow, how would you respond?

193. In your present position, what Java Web Developer problems have you identified that had previously been overlooked?

194. Why should we give you this Java Web Developer job?

195. Tell me about your salary expectations.

196. Where else have you interviewed at?

197. Tell us about a Java Web Developer decision that you made, which you knew would be unpopular with a group of people. How did you handle the Java Web Developer decision-making process and how did you manage expectations?

198. What do your subordinates think of you?

199. Tell me about a time when you had to give someone difficult Java Web Developer feedback. How did you

handle it?

200. Where do you see yourself in 2 Java Web Developer years time?

201. What can you offer us that someone else can not?

202. How would you describe the Java Web Developer pace at which you work?

203. Describe a Java Web Developer situation where you were able to influence others on an important issue. What approaches or strategies did you use?

204. How would you describe your own Java Web Developer personality?

205. Are you a fast learner? How long will it take you to begin adding value?

206. Give us an Java Web Developer example where you worked in a dysfunctional team. Why was it dysfunctional and how did you attempt to change things?

207. How do you evaluate Java Web Developer success?

208. Why do you want to be a .... ?

209. What was the worst Java Web Developer day you've ever had at work and why?

210. What about this Java Web Developer job do you find exciting?

211. If you could start your Java Web Developer career again, what would you do differently?

212. Let's get specific. Tell me about your Java Web Developer job at Company ABC.

213. Had you thought of leaving your present position before? If so, what do you think held you there?

214. What will your referees say about you?

215. Your first year in this Java Web Developer industry can be very tough. Would you be willing to become a junior agent and join a team?

216. How do you ensure that every Java Web Developer member of the team is allowed to participate?

217. How do you feel about leaving all of your Java Web Developer benefits?

218. When did you last upset someone?

219. If you were an animal, which one would you want to be?

220. Which Java Web Developer decisions do you feel able to make on your own and which do you require senior support to make?

221. Why do you want to leave your current Java Web Developer job?

222. Name one person, alive or dead, that you would

want to meet and why?

223. What would your ideal Java Web Developer job be?

224. Would you describe yourself as competitive?

225. What do you like to do in your spare time?

226. Would you work Java Web Developer holidays/weekends?

227. How have you changed the Java Web Developer nature of your job?

228. Can you work under Java Web Developer pressure?

229. Give an Java Web Developer example where you delegated a task to the wrong person? How did you make that decision at the time, what happened and what did you learn from it?

230. What Java Web Developer steps do you take to understand your colleagues' personalities? Give an example where you found it hard to adjust to one particular colleague.

231. How do you use different Java Web Developer communication tools in different situations?

232. What do you know about us - or - What do we do?

233. Describe your strongest and your weakest

colleagues. How do you cope with such Java Web Developer diversity of personalities?

234. What Are Your Expectations Regarding Salary?

235. Tell me about using XYZ.

236. Tell me about the best Java Web Developer boss you ever had. Why did you enjoy working for them so much?

237. How Would Your Co-Workers/Managers Describe You?

238. How would you deal with an angry or irate Java Web Developer customer?

239. What is your experience with hiring and firing Java Web Developer employees?

240. If you were to rank them, what are the three traits your top performers have in common?

241. What is your superpower?

242. How do you influence people in situations where there are conflicting agendas?

243. Can you act on your own initiative?

244. What's your biggest concern about working remotely?

245. What was the most difficult Java Web Developer decision you ever had to make?

246. Were you involved in any Java Web Developer teams or societies at university?

247. Tell me how you think other people would describe you.

248. What are your Java Web Developer career goals?

249. What gets you up in the morning?

250. Tell me about a time when you made a mistake at work? How did you go about rectifying it? What did you learn from the mistake?

251. How many people did you supervise on your last Java Web Developer job?

252. What is your dream Java Web Developer job?

253. How do you bring difficult colleagues on board? Give us an Java Web Developer example where you had to do this.

254. In what Java Web Developer kind of a work environment are you most comfortable?

255. Tell me about the toughest Java Web Developer decision you had to make in the last six months.

256. What Is Your Favoured Work Java Web Developer Environment?

257. I used to work with (insert name of professional Java Web Developer contact) at your former company. Did you ever meet him while you were working there?

258. Tell us about a Java Web Developer situation where you made a decision too quickly and got it wrong. Why made you take that decision?

259. Which lead Java Web Developer generation source did you see the best ROI from?

260. Describe a Java Web Developer situation where you needed to inspire a team. What challenges did you meet and how did you achieve your objectives?

261. What would your direct reports say about you?

262. What is the most difficult Java Web Developer situation you have faced?

263. What is the toughest part of a Java Web Developer job for you?

264. What do you like and dislike about the Java Web Developer job we are discussing?

265. How quickly will we see Java Web Developer results from hiring you? Would you stake your job on achieving that result by a certain date?

266. What do you think of the last Java Web Developer company you worked for?

267. Give us an Java Web Developer example of a

situation where you didn't meet your goals or objectives.

268. Do you have at least a few months worth of living expenses in the bank?

269. Tell me about a time when you were happiest at work. Why did you feel that Java Web Developer way?

270. Tell us about a time when you had Java Web Developer trouble remaining focused on your audience. How did you handle this?

271. Have you helped reduce costs? How?

272. What was the last Java Web Developer book you've read for fun?

273. How did you learn about the opening?

274. What type of writing have you done? Give Java Web Developer examples. What makes you think that you are good at it?

275. What are your salary Java Web Developer requirements?

276. When is the last time that you have refused to make a Java Web Developer decision?

277. What would you do if one of our Java Web Developer competitors offered you a position?

278. Why were you let go from your last position?

279. Why did you choose a Java Web Developer career in …?

280. What Are Your Professional Weaknesses?

281. Tell us about a project where you achieved Java Web Developer success despite the odds being stacked against you. How did you ensure that you pulled through?

282. Do you enjoy travelling?

283. What Was Your Greatest Professional Challenge and How Did You Cope?

284. What Java Web Developer percentage of employees was brought in by current employees?

285. Tell me about a time you had someone on your Java Web Developer team who was an incredible challenge. What did you do to manage them, and how did the situation turn out?

286. What would you do if your Java Web Developer boss asked you to do something illegal?

287. Tell me what you liked best and least about working at ABC.

288. What was your salary in your last Java Web Developer job?

289. What are your co-worker pet peeves?

290. What are your biggest weaknesses?

291. How do you handle your Java Web Developer calendar and schedule? What apps/systems do you use?

292. How much does your last Java Web Developer job resemble the one you are applying for? What are the differences?

293. How long would you stay with us?

294. Why are you interested in working for [insert Java Web Developer company name here]?

295. If a client emailed you asking for something outside of your territory at the Java Web Developer company, how would you handle it?

296. What Is Your Ideal Java Web Developer Job?

297. What Java Web Developer kind of work environment do you like best?

298. (If you have been offered a Java Web Developer job) Are you going to take the Java Web Developer job?

299. What do you expect me to accomplish in the first 90 days?

300. Who was your best Java Web Developer boss and who was the worst?

301. Describe a Java Web Developer situation in which you were a member of team. What did you do to

positively contribute to it?

302. How would you fire someone?

303. Would you work 40+ Java Web Developer hours a week?

304. What are your salary Java Web Developer requirements or expectations?

305. How do you manage upwards?

306. What draws you to this Java Web Developer industry?

307. Where Do You See Yourself in 5/10/20 Java Web Developer Years?

308. (If you have applied to lots of Java Web Developer places) Why haven't you had many interviews?

309. What makes you frustrated or impatient at work?

310. What will you do if you don't get this position?

311. What Java Web Developer questions do you have for me?

312. What do you do when you sense a project is going to take longer than expected?

313. What do you find are the most difficult Java Web Developer decisions to make?

314. Tell us about the biggest change that you have had to deal with. How did you cope with it?

315. If I called your Java Web Developer boss right now and asked him/her what is an area that you could improve on, what would he/she say?

316. What is the name of our CEO?

317. Why are you looking to leave your current Java Web Developer role?

318. How many people do you think are online on Facebook in Chicago right now?

319. What are your Java Web Developer strengths and weaknesses?

320. What is your favorite Java Web Developer website?

321. What other Java Web Developer types of jobs or companies are you considering?

322. What are the major Java Web Developer reasons for your success?

323. What is the first thing you would change, if you were to start work here?

324. Tell me about a time when you disagreed with your Java Web Developer boss.

325. Give an Java Web Developer example of a time when you had to deal with a conflict within your team.

What did you do to help resolve the situation?

326. Tell us about a time when someone asked you something that you objected to. How did you handle the Java Web Developer situation?

327. Describe your dream Java Web Developer job.

328. Did your level of responsibility grow or change while you were at ABC?

329. What do you do when you are late for work?

330. What Java Web Developer environments allow you to be especially effective?

331. How did you hear about this position?

332. What are the company's highest-priority Java Web Developer goals this year, and how would my role contribute?

333. What were your objectives for last year? Did you achieve them?

334. What are three Java Web Developer things most important to you in a job?

335. What value will you bring to the position?

336. Being an Java Web Developer can be a stressful Java Web Developer job. Tell me about a time when you had to multitask a deadline, a phone ringing off the hook, and an error to fix all at the same time, or something

similar to that. What did you prioritize on this crazy day and why?

337. Are you willing to travel?

338. How do you feel about becoming Java Web Developer friends with your coworkers? Is it a good idea or a bad idea?

339. How many Java Web Developer hours are you prepared to work?

340. We're considering two other Java Web Developer candidates for this position. Why should we hire you rather than someone else?

341. How would you describe yourself?

342. If I Java Web Developer spoke with your previous boss, what would he say are your greatest strengths and weaknesses?

343. Did you feel you progressed satisfactorily in your last Java Web Developer job?

344. How do you deal with a project that's gone over Java Web Developer budget or pushed past the deadline?

345. If you could relive the last 10 Java Web Developer years of your life.

346. Before you came in, I looked at the Java Web Developer mission and vision from your current (or past) company. What is it in your own words?

347. Tell us about a time when you went against Java Web Developer company policy. Why did you do it and how did you handle it?

348. What do you think of your Java Web Developer boss?

349. Why are you applying for this position?

350. What was the hardest Java Web Developer decision you have ever had to make?

351. You walk into the Java Web Developer office and have 8 emails and 4 voicemails from clients before your day has even started, all with different urgent requests. What do you do?

352. How do you plan to achieve those Java Web Developer goals?

353. Discuss your resume.

354. What do you like the most and least about working in this Java Web Developer industry?

355. How has your Java Web Developer education prepared you for your career?

356. Do you prefer to work in a small, medium or large Java Web Developer company?

357. As a Java Web Developer manager in this role, you will be responsible for leading a team of X people. What specifically will you do during year one to help ensure they each become more valuable to the company and stronger performers overall?

358. Do we have your Java Web Developer permission to verify your employment eligibility and do employment/background checks?

359. Are you a Java Web Developer leader or a follower?

360. Do you prefer working in a Java Web Developer team or on your own?

361. Where do you see yourself in five Java Web Developer years?

362. When did you make a Java Web Developer decision that wasn't yours to make?

363. What do you find most challenging when you accompany prospective Java Web Developer clients on showings? Why?

364. How would you feel about re-locating?

365. Tell me about the last time a co-worker or Java Web Developer customer got angry with you. What happened?

366. What Java Web Developer problems has one of your staff or colleagues brought to you recently? How did you assist them?

367. What Java Web Developer career options do you have at the moment?

368. How would you feel about frequent travel?

369. How do you prioritize Java Web Developer tasks?

370. What do your work colleagues think of you?

371. Where do you see yourself in 5 Java Web Developer years? 10 Java Web Developer years?

372. How do you plan the writing of a report?

373. Tell me about a time when you took a risk... How did you handle it?

374. Tell me about at least one significant Java Web Developer career achievement.

375. Tell us about a Java Web Developer situation where you trusted your team to derive a new approach to an old problem. How did you manage the process?

376. What are your salary Java Web Developer requirements? (Hint: if you're not sure what's a fair salary range and compensation package, research the job title and/or company on Glassdoor.)

377. What is your dream Java Web Developer job? Describe it to me.

378. What do you plan to do if...?

379. Can you show me Java Web Developer proof of ROI (return on investment) on marketing campaign(s) that you've led, designed, or otherwise participated in, as

well as what lessons, both good and bad, you learned from them?

380. How do you ensure compliance with policies in your Java Web Developer area of responsibility?

381. Are there any Java Web Developer tasks or jobs you feel are beneath you?

382. What do you consider to be your biggest professional achievement?

383. Tell us about a project or Java Web Developer situation where you felt that the conventional approach would not be suitable. How did you derive and manage a new approach? Which challenges did you face and how did you address them?

384. What is your ideal work schedule in regards to flex-time and in-Java Web Developer office and remote working?

385. Are you willing to relocate?

386. What is the single most important Java Web Developer factor that would make you happy in your job that is not from the job itself?

387. Discuss your educational Java Web Developer background.

388. Why did you choose this particular Java Web Developer career path?

389. Describe a Java Web Developer situation where

you needed to influence different stakeholders who had different agendas. What approaches or strategies did you use?

390. What really drives Java Web Developer results in this job?

391. What is your biggest Java Web Developer weakness?

392. What was the biggest challenge you ever faced?

393. How would you describe the Java Web Developer essence of success? According to your definition of success, how successful have you been so far?

394. Describe a Java Web Developer situation where you had to drive a team through change. How did you achieve this?

395. What is your worst selling experience?

396. How would you manage a project with a lot of Java Web Developer steps and a lot of people?

397. What are your Java Web Developer career goals? How will you get there?

398. What positive and negative Java Web Developer feedback have you received about your writing skills? Give an example where one of your reports was criticised.

399. How much Java Web Developer money did you account for?

400. What do you know about our Java Web Developer company?

401. Do you like working with figures more than Java Web Developer words?

402. Tell me a little about yourself.

403. Why do you want to work remotely?

404. What Is Your Greatest Professional Achievement To Date?

405. What was the last Java Web Developer book you read? Movie you saw? Sporting event you attended?

406. Have you ever worked in a Java Web Developer situation when there was no processes or procedures in place?

407. Why do you want to work for this Java Web Developer company?

408. What gets your fired up and leaping out of bed in the morning?

409. Which change of Java Web Developer job did you find the most difficult to make?

410. Which recent project or Java Web Developer situation has caused you the most stress? How did you deal with it?

411. What about the Java Web Developer job offered do

you find the most attractive? Least attractive?

412. Tell us about a Java Web Developer situation where conflict led to a negative outcome. How did you handle the Java Web Developer situation and what did you learn from it?

413. What would you say are your strong Java Web Developer points?

414. Tell us about a Java Web Developer situation where things deteriorated quickly. How did you react to recover from that Java Web Developer situation?

415. How much do you know about our Java Web Developer company, products and services?

416. Why haven't you applied to more firms?

417. What was your biggest setback?

418. Why Is There A Java Web Developer Gap In Your Employment?

419. How do you feel writing a report differs from preparing an oral Java Web Developer presentation?

420. Tell us about a time when you felt that conflict or differences were a positive driving force in your Java Web Developer organization. How did handle the conflict to optimise its benefit?

421. Why are you looking for a new Java Web Developer job?

422. Which course or Java Web Developer topics have you found most difficult? How did you address the challenge?

423. What Java Web Developer challenges and opportunities do you think the company faces?

424. Why do you want to work for us?

425. Can You Tell Me About Yourself?

426. If I called your Java Web Developer boss right now and asked him what is an area that you could improve on, what would he say?

427. How do you deal with adversity?

428. What Java Web Developer questions haven't I asked you?

429. How much do you expect if we offer this position to you?

430. Are you overqualified for this Java Web Developer job?

431. Why are you leaving (did you leave) ABC?

432. Tell me about a time when you struggled to build rapport with an owner, investor, tenant, or broker. What would you have done differently?

433. Why did you choose your Java Web Developer university and what factors influenced your choice?

434. How did you build up your own personal social media channels and online presence? What do you think works or does not work?

435. Why have you made so many Java Web Developer applications?

436. What type of responsibilities do you Java Web Developer delegate? Give examples of projects where you made best use of delegation.

437. How do you see this position assisting you in achieving your Java Web Developer career goals?

438. Tell us about a time when you had to convince a senior Java Web Developer colleague that change was necessary. What made you think that your new approach would be better suited?

439. What do you know about this Java Web Developer company?

440. Give a time when you went above and beyond the Java Web Developer requirements for a project.

441. Are you a Java Web Developer leader? (Java Web Developer leadership)

442. What scares you the most in Java Web Developer life?

443. Describe a Java Web Developer situation where you had a disagreement or an argument with a superior. How did you handle it?

444. Tell us about a Java Web Developer situation where you had to get a team to improve its performance. What were the problems and how did you address them?

445. Tell me about a special Java Web Developer contribution you have made to your employer.

446. How do you process Java Web Developer information??

447. Would your current Java Web Developer boss describe you as the type of person who goes that extra mile?

448. What Java Web Developer kind of salary are you worth?

449. Why do you want to work for our Java Web Developer company in this role?

450. How many Java Web Developer applications have you made?

451. Describe the last significant conflict you had at work and how you handled it?

452. Why do you think you'd be the right administrative assistant for me/for this Java Web Developer office?

453. If you owned the Java Web Developer company, what would you change?

454. Why do you want to leave your current Java Web Developer company?

455. Tell me about a time when you demonstrated Java Web Developer leadership and initiative?

456. What would your first 30, 60, and 90 Java Web Developer day plans look like in this role?

457. Can you work under pressures, deadlines, etc.?

458. Are you prepared to relocate?

459. What is the biggest risk that you have taken? How did you handle the process?

460. Tell us about Java Web Developer risks that you have taken in your professional or personal life. How did you go about making your decision?

461. Have you ever been in a difficult Java Web Developer situation when you needed to remain positive? How did you handle it?

462. Why was there a Java Web Developer gap in your employment between [insert date] and [insert date]?

Motivation and Values

1. Are there specific times you cannot work?

2. Would your spouse object if you traveled or worked overtime?

3. Tell me about a time when you worked under close Java Web Developer supervision or extremely loose Java Web Developer supervision. How did you handle that?

4. What is your greatest strength or Java Web Developer weakness?

5. Tell me about a time you were dissatisfied in your work. What could have been done to make it better?

6. The school is the place you did most of your formal learning. What is it about the school and the Java Web Developer way it is organised that encouraged you to attend?

7. Do you feel you make a Java Web Developer difference?

8. Can you think of products, ads, or brands that are anti-materialistic?

9. How many Java Web Developer hours did you spend dedicated to a task before you attained your current level of proficiency?

10. What Java Web Developer steps did you go through in accomplishing your most recent project?

11. How could you have organized your Java Web Developer information differently?

12. How do you stay up to date in your Java Web Developer skills? Give me examples.

13. Do you get ill from stress?

14. If your Java Web Developer memory was wiped and you had to read one book to regain your perspective, which would it be?

15. Over a several month Java Web Developer period, you realize that a number of auto thefts have occurred in the parking lot. What type of actions might you consider to address the problem?

16. What makes you excited to go to work, and why?

17. What do you want to do?

18. How would you define 'Java Web Developer success' for someone in your chosen career?

19. What's your favorite thing about marketing? And why do you love it?

20. Give me an Java Web Developer example of a time when you went above and beyond the call of duty

21. Can you perform (any or all of the Java Web Developer job functions) with or without accommodation?

22. What have you done to prepare yourself for today?

23. What's the ONE thing you need for your next position to be the best Java Web Developer job experience of your life?

24. Describe a time when you saw some Java Web Developer problem and took the initiative to correct it rather than waiting for someone else to do it.

25. How can our Java Web Developer company increase employee engagement and retain top performers?

26. What is your current Java Web Developer life goal is and where do you want to end up?

27. List the core Java Web Developer values you believe are necessary when teaching in a school serving a disadvantaged community?

28. Tell me about a time when you had to deliver some unpleasant or sensitive Java Web Developer information to someone. How did you handle the situation?

29. This Java Web Developer job requires a lot of stamina. How do you think you will be able to withstand these rigors?

30. In 2026, how do you envision Personal Java Web Developer Data Fusion making you smarter?

31. What Java Web Developer steps did you take to calm

things down?

32. Give an Java Web Developer example of a time when you had to be relatively quick in coming to a decision. How did it turn out?

33. Tell us about a time when you had to make a difficult Java Web Developer decision. What was the situation, what did you do about it, and what was the outcome?

34. What language(s) do you read, speak or write fluently?

35. Which one of the following three Java Web Developer things motivates you most: sense of ownership, intellectual curiosity, or collaborating with peers?

36. Have you ever been hurt on the Java Web Developer job?

37. Would you be able and willing to work overtime as necessary?

38. When you look back in a year from now and I bump into you at our holiday Java Web Developer party, how you will have known that working here was a good decision and what would you tell me?

39. When was the last time you had to work hard to accomplish something seemingly insurmountable where the odds were stacked against you?

40. What is your personal Java Web Developer mission, and how does this job description align with that Java

Web Developer mission?

41. If we hire you right now, what are you doing at our Java Web Developer company tomorrow, and what will you be doing at our Java Web Developer company one year from now?

42. Who is someone you aspire to be like, and why?

43. Give me an Java Web Developer example of a time you were able to be creative with your work. What was exciting or difficult about it?

44. What were the easiest subjects in school for you?

45. Tell me about your proudest professional Java Web Developer accomplishment.

46. There is a movement away from materialism in our Java Web Developer culture. Can you think of products, ads, or brands that are anti-materialistic?

47. What motivates you to stay?

48. What child care arrangements have you made?

49. Do you have responsibilities other than work that will interfere with specific Java Web Developer job requirements such as traveling or working overtime?

50. What do you want to be known for?

51. In which aspects do you excel?

52. Have you ever filed for workers compensation?

53. Describe a time when you were confronted with an angry Java Web Developer customer, supervisor or coworker. How did you react?

54. Do sources of thriving apply to your own Java Web Developer life and work, or people you know?

55. Tell us me about an important Java Web Developer goal that you set in the past. Were you successful? Why?

56. What Java Web Developer kind of stress were you under and from where?

57. How many sick days did you take last year?

58. If you woke up tomorrow a billionaire and never had to work another Java Web Developer day for the rest of your life, what would you do?

59. Describe the Java Web Developer task you had to accomplish. What were your responsibilities in this situation?

60. Give an Java Web Developer example of a time when you went above and beyond the call of duty

61. What do you want to be most remembered for when you move on from this Java Web Developer role?

62. Describe a Java Web Developer situation when you were able to have a positive influence on the actions of others

63. Finishing up your Junior summer, heading into your senior year, what were you thinking about plans for after graduation?

64. How do you handle stress?

65. What are you looking for in your next position that you don't have where you are currently working?

66. Do you work better or worse under Java Web Developer pressure?

67. Where were you born?

68. What would you do if you were given an assignment but no instruction on how to perform the duties involved?

69. What do you do to cope with stress?

70. What do you think are the 3 -5 core Java Web Developer values that best describe you today?

71. Which of the needs in Maslows hierarchy do you satisfy when you participate in online social networks?

72. Will you be able to work on weekends or Java Web Developer holidays as the job requires?

73. What obstacles did you encounter, and how did you overcome them?

Outgoingness

1. How do you know if your Java Web Developer customers are satisfied?

2. Tell us about a time when you delayed responding to a Java Web Developer situation until you had time to review the facts, even though there was pressure to act quickly.

3. Being Java Web Developer successful is hard work. Tell us about a specific achievement when you had to work especially hard to attain the Java Web Developer success you desired.

4. On occasion, we have to be firm and assertive in order to achieve a desired result. Tell us about a time when you had to do that.

5. There are times when we need to insist on doing something a certain Java Web Developer way. Give us the details surrounding a situation when you had to insist on doing something "your Java Web Developer way". What was the outcome?

6. Have you ever had Java Web Developer difficulty getting along with co-workers? How did you handle the situation and what was the outcome?

7. Describe some particularly trying Java Web Developer customer complaints or resistance you have had to handle. How did you react? What was the outcome?

8. In Java Web Developer job situations you may be pulled in many different directions at once. Tell us about

a time when you had to respond to this type of situation. How did you manage yourself?

9. Tell us about a time when you were effective in handling a Java Web Developer customer complaint. Why were you effective? What was the outcome?

10. Tell us about a time when you had to motivate a Java Web Developer group of people to get an important job done. What did you do, what was the outcome?

11. Sooner or later we all have to deal with a Java Web Developer customer who has unreasonable demands. Think of a time when you had to handle unreasonable requests. What did you do and what was the outcome?

12. Describe a time when you were able to effectively communicate a difficult or unpleasant Java Web Developer idea to a superior.

13. Many of us have had co-workers or managers who tested our patience. Tell us about a time when you restrained yourself to avoid conflict with a co-worker or supervisor. (restrained)

Project Management

1. Tell us about a time when you Java Web Developer influenced the outcome of a project by taking a leadership role

2. Using a specific Java Web Developer example of a project, tell how you kept those involved informed of the progress

Setting Performance Standards

1. How do you let subordinates know what you expect of them?

2. What Java Web Developer performance standards do you have for your unit? How have you communicated them to your subordinates?

3. How do you go about setting Java Web Developer goals with subordinates? How do you involve them in this process?

Values Diversity

1. Tell us about a time that you successfully adapted to a culturally different Java Web Developer environment

2. Tell us about a time when you made an intentional Java Web Developer effort to get to know someone from another culture

3. What have you done to support Java Web Developer diversity in your unit?

4. What measures have you taken to make someone feel comfortable in an Java Web Developer environment that was obviously uncomfortable with his or her presence?

5. Give a specific Java Web Developer example of how you have helped create an environment where differences are valued, encouraged and supported

6. Tell us about a time when you had to adapt to a wide Java Web Developer variety of people by accepting/ understanding their perspective

7. What have you done to further your Java Web Developer knowledge/understanding about diversity? How have you demonstrated your learning?

Behavior

1. Were you honorably discharged?

2. Pick any event in the last five Java Web Developer years of your work which gives a good example of your ability to use forecasting techniques. Did you use statistical procedures or a gut level approach?

3. Have you ever faced a Java Web Developer problem you could not solve?

4. Describe a time when you put your needs aside to help a co-worker understand a Java Web Developer task. How did you assist him or her?

5. What were your favorite courses?

6. What was your rank at time of discharge?

7. Why do you think you would be good at this Java Web Developer job

8. Are you comfortable about working on many Java Web Developer projects at once?

9. What disabilities and Java Web Developer challenges (physical, mental, emotional, or behavioral) can you comfortably handle?

10. Tell me about a time when your attempt to motivate a person/Java Web Developer group was rejected. What have you done to remotivate a demoralized team/person?

11. How would you resolve a Java Web Developer

customer service problem where the Java Web Developer customer demanded an immediate refund?

12. Give me an Java Web Developer example of a group decision you were involved with recently. What part did you play in helping the group develop the final decision?

13. Tell me about a time when you had to take care of an upset Java Web Developer customer?

14. What processes have you used to build a Java Web Developer team?

15. Can you tell me about a Java Web Developer job experience in which you had to speak up and tell other people what you thought or felt?

16. Describe a time when you had to adopt a well-defined work Java Web Developer routine. How long did the situation last?

17. What Java Web Developer problem were you trying to solve?

18. Why did you leave your last position?

19. Tell me about the most frustrating thing you ever had to deal with?

20. What rewards are most important to you in your Java Web Developer career and why?

21. How have you positively changed in the workplace to adapt to your colleagues or supervisor?

22. How many days were you absent last year?

23. How have your extracurricular Java Web Developer activities and/or work experience prepared you for work in our company?

24. Tell me about times when you seized the opportunities, grabbed something and ran with it yourself. Have you ever started something up from nothing – give an Java Web Developer example?

25. Have you had to convince a Java Web Developer team to work on a project they werent thrilled about?

26. Describe a specific Java Web Developer problem you solved for your employer. How did you approach the Java Web Developer problem?

27. What are your strong Java Web Developer points?

28. Who was your best client?

29. How many people live in your household?

30. Can you describe a time when your work was criticized?

31. Tell us about a time that others Java Web Developer actions negatively impacted a project for which you were responsible. What did you do?

32. When do you plan to retire?

33. Has your Java Web Developer manager / supervisor / team leader ever asked you to do something that you didnt think was appropriate?

34. Were you discharged under honorable or other acceptable Java Web Developer conditions?

35. Have you ever dealt with Java Web Developer company policy you werent in agreement with?

36. What are your Java Web Developer career interests?

37. Based on your prior work, what Java Web Developer ideas for improvement do you have?

38. To what extent did a project test your comprehension Java Web Developer skills and technical knowledge?

39. What is your typical Java Web Developer way of dealing with conflict?

40. Tell me about the last time you had to smooth over a disagreement between two other people. What was the end result?

41. How do you rate yourself in Java Web Developer terms of creativity in the fields of art, writing, and music?

42. Did you take Java Web Developer action IMMEDIATELY or are you more DELIBERATE and slow?

43. What are your Java Web Developer career plans (short and long range)?

44. Would you be able and willing to travel as needed on this Java Web Developer job?

45. What significant changes do you foresee in the Java Web Developer company / organization?

46. What Java Web Developer communication strengths do you have that make you suited for this type of work?

47. Did you ever not meet your Java Web Developer goals?

48. Have you ever over-Java Web Developer planned a project or spent too much time in planning versus execution?

49. What would be the best Java Web Developer example that shows you are an honest person?

50. If you think about when you need high Java Web Developer performance, what behavior do you fall back on?

51. Tell me about a time when you came up with an innovative Java Web Developer solution to a challenge your company / organization was facing. What was the challenge?

52. What did you do that was particularly effective / ineffective?

53. Have you ever taken a stand or said something in

public that you knew those above you would not like?

54. How does your graduate school experience relate to this Java Web Developer job?

55. Do you have children at home?

56. Tell me about a time when you had to give someone difficult Java Web Developer feedback. How did you handle it?

57. Describe how your position contributes to your organizations/units Java Web Developer goals. What are the units Java Web Developer goals/mission?

58. Is there any Java Web Developer day of the week youre not able to work?

59. How would you deal with an angry Java Web Developer customer?

60. How do you handle stress and Java Web Developer pressure on the job?

61. What do you wish to avoid in your next Java Web Developer job?

62. What Can You Do for Us That Other Java Web Developer Candidates Cant?

63. What Java Web Developer skills do you bring to the job?

64. How would your past supervisors describe you?

65. When have you been most proud of your ability to wait for important Java Web Developer information before taking action in solving a problem?

66. What are you looking for in your next Java Web Developer career opportunity?

67. Tell me about a time when you postponed making a Java Web Developer decision. Why did you?

68. What are your greatest Java Web Developer strengths?

69. Do you own a car?

70. What does your spouse do for a living?

71. Whats the origin of your name?

72. How many times have you totally altered behavior or belief in response to one persuasive Java Web Developer effort?

73. What are the most challenging documents you have done?

74. Can you give me an Java Web Developer example of how you have persuaded executives to see your point of view in the past?

75. How do you know whether its better to lay out very specifically what others have to do – versus allowing them to use their own initiative and creativity?

76. Tell me about the duties and responsibilities of your

current/last position?

77. Give me an Java Web Developer example of a time that you felt you went above and beyond the call of duty at work.

78. Describe your ideal Java Web Developer candidate?

79. Give me an Java Web Developer example of when you had to show good leadership?

80. What computer software programs are you familiar with?

81. Describe how you would handle a Java Web Developer situation if you were required to finish multiple tasks by the end of the day, and there was no conceivable way that you could finish them.

82. What are you personally looking for in a successful Java Web Developer candidate?

83. When have you found yourself in my position?

84. In your position as _____, how did you determine which duties to Java Web Developer delegate to subordinates?

85. Time Java Web Developer management has become a necessary factor in personal productivity. Give me an example of any Time Java Web Developer management skill you have learned and applied at work. What resulted from use of the skill?

86. Why are you better suited for this position than other Java Web Developer candidates?

87. What is your name?

88. Tell me about a time where you had to deal with conflict on the Java Web Developer job.

89. Tell me about a Java Web Developer customer whose needs you spent considerable time learning about. What was the result of the time investment?

90. Do you have any health Java Web Developer problems?

91. Tell Me About Yourself?

92. Tell me about a time when you failed to meet a deadline. What Java Web Developer things did you fail to do?

93. What are your Java Web Developer strengths, weaknesses, interests and career goals?

94. Can you tell us about a time when you needed to be particularly sensitive to another persons beliefs, cultural Java Web Developer background, or way of doing things?

95. Did you have a strategic plan?

96. Tell me about a time when you were successful in this Java Web Developer area-what kind of payoffs accrued to yourself, the other individual, and the organization?

97. What part did you play in helping a Java Web Developer group develop a final decision?

98. What are your greatest achievements at this point in your Java Web Developer life?

99. Can you tell us about a really difficult Java Web Developer decision you had to make at work recently?

100. What is the worst mistake you ever made?

101. How would you describe your Java Web Developer management style?

102. Do you feel that you have experienced a Behavioral Based Java Web Developer Interview yet?

103. How do you track your progress so that you can meet deadlines?

104. How much alcohol do you drink each week?

105. Give me a specific Java Web Developer example of a time when you had to address an angry customer. What was the problem and what was the outcome?

106. How has your previous experience prepared you for the duties of this position?

107. Tell me about the most creative thing you ve ever done?

108. Have you ever led a research Java Web Developer team in a formal manner?

109. What type of Java Web Developer system did you use?

110. What specific Java Web Developer goals have you established for your career?

111. What has been your most significant work related disappointment?

112. Tell me about a time when you handled an arrogant person or one who made you angry. What is your typical Java Web Developer way of dealing with conflict?

113. How would you describe the quality and quantity of his/her work?

114. Can you tell us about a time when you formed an ongoing working Java Web Developer relationship or partnership with someone from another organization to achieve a mutual goal?

115. How did you decide on your major?

116. If you found out your Java Web Developer company was doing something against the law, like fraud, what would you do?

117. Were you ever a union Java Web Developer member?

118. What Are Three Positive Java Web Developer Things Your Last Supervisor Would Say About You?

119. Ive given you a short overview of the Java Web

Developer job, but is there anything else that youd like to ask about?

120. How did you prepare for this?

121. Java Web Developer Jobs differ in the extent to which unexpected changes can disrupt daily responsibilities. How do you feel when this happens?

122. Have you ever had your wages garnished?

123. What would be the best Java Web Developer example that shows you are a person of integrity?

124. Why Did You Leave (Are You Leaving) Your Java Web Developer Job?

125. Tell me about a time you had to say no to a Java Web Developer customer?

126. What language do you speak at home?

127. What's the most difficult Java Web Developer decision you've made in the last two years and how did you come to that Java Web Developer decision?

128. Are you bilingual?

129. Give an Java Web Developer example of when you questioned the way things have always been done to ensure that a process continued to be relevant and add value. What was the outcome?

130. Analyze your own Java Web Developer background.

What skills do you have (content, functional, and adaptive) that relate to your job objective?

131. What Java Web Developer skills do you have (content, functional, and adaptive) that relate to your job objective?

132. What major Java Web Developer accomplishment would you like to achieve in your life and why?

133. Have you gone above and beyond the call of duty?

134. Tell me about a Java Web Developer situation in which you worked with your direct reports/team members to develop new and creative ideas to solve a business problem. What problem were you trying to solve?

135. Tell me about the last time you had to sell your Java Web Developer ideas to others. What did you do that was particularly effective/ineffective?

136. Tell me about a time you had a particularly difficult Java Web Developer problem to solve. What was the Java Web Developer problem, how did you solve it, or what was the result?

137. Some people consider themselves to be big Java Web Developer picture people and others are detail oriented. Which are you?

138. Whats the most recent mistake you made, and why did you make it?

139. When did you graduate from high school?

140. Tell me about a Java Web Developer situation in which you were particularly skillful in detecting clues which show how another person thinks or feels. How did you size up the person?

141. Have you ever had to present an unpopular proposal/point of view that you believed in?

142. Often individuals who are creative in one mode seem to have creative Java Web Developer skills in other areas. How do you rate yourself in terms of creativity in the fields of art, writing, and music?

143. What was the most difficult Java Web Developer period in your life, and how did you deal with it?

144. What was the best Java Web Developer idea you had for improving the way things were done on your last job?

145. What would you do if an employee called in sick three Mondays in a row?

146. Give an Java Web Developer example of a time when you made a mistake. How did you handle it?

147. Why Do You Want to Work Here?

148. Describe a time when you had to influence a number of different constituents with differing interests. What Java Web Developer kind of influencing techniques did you use?

149. Take us through a complicated project you were responsible for planning. How did you define and measure Java Web Developer success?

150. What clubs, lodges do you belong to?

151. What was the last project you led, and what was its Java Web Developer outcome?

152. What situations do you find most frustrating?

153. Where do you live?

154. Would you be able to meet this requirement?

155. When you worked on multiple Java Web Developer projects how did you prioritize?

156. Have you ever been on a Java Web Developer team where someone was not pulling their own weight? How did you handle it?

157. Is there something in this Java Web Developer job that you hope to accomplish that you were not able to accomplish in your last Java Web Developer job?

158. What were your most significant accomplishments in your prior work experience?

159. How do you motivate others to do a particularly good Java Web Developer job?

160. I have a Java Web Developer job. I have a career. Im on a mission. Whats the difference between those three statements, and which one applies to you?

161. Can you travel?

162. How did your planning help you deal with the unexpected?

163. What Java Web Developer types of experience have you had in managing situations that involve human health/human welfare or severe financial outcomes?

164. Did you use statistical Java Web Developer procedures or a gut level approach?

165. Tell me about a Java Web Developer suggestion you made to improve the way job processes or operations worked. What was the result?

166. Did you do anything specific to deal with the stress?

167. What were the Java Web Developer Results of your actions?

168. When have you found it necessary to use detailed checklists/Java Web Developer procedures to reduce potential for error on the job?

169. What interests you most about this Java Web Developer job?

170. Have you received any _____?

171. Select a Java Web Developer job you have had and describe the paperwork you were required to complete. What specific things did you do to ensure your accuracy?

172. Have you ever been arrested?

173. What made your Java Web Developer communication effective?

174. When has it been necessary for you to tolerate an ambiguous Java Web Developer situation at work?

175. Are you for or against unions?

176. How many children do you have?

177. Give me a specific Java Web Developer example of a time when you sold your supervisor or professor on an idea or concept. How did you proceed?

178. How do you react to criticism?

179. How do you keep your Java Web Developer staff informed of what s going on in the organization?

180. What was one of the worst Java Web Developer communication problems you have experienced?

181. Give me an Java Web Developer example of a time you did something wrong. How did you handle it?

182. What would you say about your ability to work in an ambiguous or unstructured circumstance?

183. What do you do if you disagree with your Java Web Developer boss?

184. What prompted your interest in our position?

185. Describe a time when you were faced with Java Web Developer problems or stresses at work that tested your coping skills. What did you do?

186. In what areas do you find yourself procrastinating?

187. What are your Java Web Developer strengths/weaknesses?

188. What was the most complex assignment you have had?

189. Tell me about your current top priorities. How did you determine that they should be your top priorities?

190. Have you had any personal, domestic or financial Java Web Developer problems that interfered with your work?

191. How did you know established methods wouldnt work?

192. Are you decisive on the Java Web Developer job?

193. What was the most stressful Java Web Developer situation at work that you have faced?

194. How did you ensure that the other person understood?

195. We all have to make Java Web Developer decisions on the job about the delicate balance between personal and work objectives. When do you feel you have had to make personal sacrifices in order to get the job done?

196. Give an Java Web Developer example of when you planned how to eliminate unnecessary activities and procedures in order to improve efficiency and make better use of resources. What was the outcome of your efforts?

197. What assignment was too difficult for you, and how did you resolve the Java Web Developer issue?

198. Can you perform these Java Web Developer tasks?

199. What was the most difficult Java Web Developer decision you have made in the last year?

200. If I were your supervisor and asked you to do something that you disagreed with, what would you do?

201. Tell me about a time when you had more on you plate than you could handle. How did you get everything accomplished?

202. What prior work experience have you had and how

does it relate to this Java Web Developer job?

203. What did you do or say to resolve a Java Web Developer situation?

204. What will it take to attain your Java Web Developer goals, and what steps have you taken toward attaining them?

205. Why are you interested in this particular Java Web Developer company?

206. Describe a Java Web Developer problem you worked on as a team member ?

207. Aside from your formal academic Java Web Developer education, can you think of something you have done to grow professionally in the recent past?

208. Give me an Java Web Developer example of a time when you used a systematic process to define your objectives. What type of system did you use?

209. What Java Web Developer kinds of decisions do you make rapidly and which ones to you take more time on?

210. Why should you hire you?

211. What are your Java Web Developer career goals in the next 3-5 years?

212. Describe the most difficult Java Web Developer team you worked on, what was your role, and what knowledge have you applied?

213. What sources would you use to research a Java Web Developer company for a potential job interview?

214. What do you see yourself doing in ten Java Web Developer years?

215. Have you found Java Web Developer ways to make your job easier?

216. What makes you unique?

217. What motivates you to put forth your greatest Java Web Developer effort?

218. Describe a recent Java Web Developer problem in which you included your subordinates in arriving at a solution?

219. Tell me about a time when you faced frustration. How did you deal with it?

220. How many Java Web Developer employees did you supervise in your last job?

221. Describe the Java Web Developer system you use for keeping track of multiple projects. How do you track your progress so that you can meet deadlines?

222. Recall a time from your work experience when your Java Web Developer manager or supervisor was unavailable and a problem arose. What was the nature of the problem?

223. Do you prefer to work independently or on a Java

Web Developer team?

224. Tell me about the specific times in which you have initiated your own Java Web Developer goal setting over the last few years. What happened?

225. Describe a time when you were expected to act in accordance with Java Web Developer policy even when it was not convenient. What did you do?

226. Why are you interested in this position?

227. What is the biggest mistake youve made?

228. What did you do in your last Java Web Developer job to contribute toward a teamwork environment?

229. Where do you want to be five Java Web Developer years from now?

230. What additional Java Web Developer information would you like me to provide?

231. What Java Web Developer effort does handling many things simultaneously have on you?

232. What do you expect from a Java Web Developer manager?

233. Describe a significant project Java Web Developer idea you initiated in the last year. How did you know it was needed?

234. If you could relive your Java Web Developer college experiences, what would you do differently?

235. Can you tell us about a Java Web Developer situation where you found it challenging to build a trusting relationship with another individual?

236. How do you determine or evaluate Java Web Developer success?

237. What s your availability for employment?

238. How did you organize the work you needed to do?

239. If you could create your ideal Java Web Developer job, what Java Web Developer job would you create?

240. Tell me about a Java Web Developer task or project that you unsuccessfully delegated. What happened?

241. What Java Web Developer things did you fail to do?

242. Describe the Java Web Developer types of teams youve been involved with. What were your roles?

243. How would you organize your Java Web Developer friends to help you move into a new apartment?

244. Where does your spouse work?

245. Tell me about the most difficult or uncooperative person you had to work with lately. What did you do or

say to resolve the Java Web Developer situation?

246. If you were at a Java Web Developer business lunch and you ordered a rare steak and they brought it to you well done, what would you do?

247. What Java Web Developer steps do you take in preparing for a meeting where you are attempting to persuade someone on a specific course of action?

248. Make a list of your selling Java Web Developer points. What are your strengths, weaknesses, interests and career goals?

249. What is your Java Web Developer idea of the perfect job?

250. To what extent has your past work required you to be skilled in the analysis of technical reports or Java Web Developer information?

251. Have you ever been on welfare?

252. Describe what Java Web Developer steps/methods you have used to define/identify a vision for your unit/position. How do you see your job relating to the overall goals of the organization?

253. Did you ever serve in the armed forces of another country?

254. When were you born?

255. Give an Java Web Developer example of how

you worked effectively with people to accomplish an important result. Have you ever been a project leader?

256. Have you had any prior work injuries?

257. Describe a Java Web Developer situation where others you were working with on a project disagreed with your ideas. What did you do?

258. Could you share with us recent Java Web Developer accomplishment of which you were particularly proud?

259. Have you ever worked on a project outside your Java Web Developer area of expertise?

260. Can you do this?

261. How would you describe yourself in Java Web Developer terms of your ability to work as a member of a team?

262. Tell me about a time you had to juggle a number of work priorities. What did you do?

263. What important Java Web Developer target dates did you set to reach objectives on your last job?

264. How would you address an angry Java Web Developer customer?

265. Do you have any back Java Web Developer problems?

266. What has been your experience in working with

conflicting, delayed, or ambiguous Java Web Developer information?

267. Cite an Java Web Developer example where you had to delegate authority?

268. Describe a time when you were asked to complete a difficult Java Web Developer task or project where the odds were against you. Were you successful?

269. How did you decide on how should you dress for the Java Web Developer interview?

270. How Do You Know When You ve Got It Right?

271. What is your timetable for achievement of your current Java Web Developer career goals?

272. Has poor motivation on someone elses part ever damaged anything you were trying to accomplish?

273. Did you have a chance to apply what you learned on the Java Web Developer job?

274. How do you go about establishing rapport with a student or Java Web Developer customer?

275. What did you like most about your last Java Web Developer job?

276. If you had to describe yourself, what Java Web Developer words would you use?

277. What is your initial reaction to change?

278. Can you give us an Java Web Developer example of when your curiosity made a real difference in a product or project?

279. How do you handle working with people who annoy you?

280. Tell me about a time you had to handle multiple responsibilities. How did you organize the work you needed to do?

281. Describe the biggest challenge you ever faced?

282. What characteristics would you be looking for in the successful Java Web Developer job applicant?

283. When do you feel you have had to make personal sacrifices in order to get the Java Web Developer job done?

284. What are the most common forms of political behavior that you see in your work Java Web Developer environment?

285. Describe a time when politics at work affected your Java Web Developer job. How did you handle the situation?

286. Did you every make a risky Java Web Developer decision?

287. How many days were you out sick last year?

288. How would you evaluate your technical Java Web Developer skills?

289. Describe for me your most recent Java Web Developer group effort?

290. What are some of the objectives you would like accomplished in the next two or three months?

291. How can you start preparing now?

292. What, if anything, did you do to mitigate the negative consequences to people?

293. What would you do if an angry 4-H client came in the door?

294. Did you use any tools such as research, brainstorming, or mathematics?

295. Describe the last time you organized a project on the Java Web Developer job?

296. Describe some times when you were not very satisfied or pleased with your Java Web Developer performance. What did you do about it?

297. How have you broken the ice in a first conversation with a Java Web Developer customer?

298. Have you ever designed a Java Web Developer program which dealt with taking quicker action?

299. What was your greatest Java Web Developer success in using the principles of logic to solve technical

problems at work?

300. What else could you do to calm an angry Java Web Developer customer?

301. Describe a time when you went the extra mile for a Java Web Developer customer?

302. Can you recall a particularly stressful Java Web Developer situation you have had at work recently?

303. Please tell me about accomplishments in your academic Java Web Developer program that are relevant to your future career goals?

304. Give me a specific Java Web Developer example of a time when a co-worker or criticized your work in front of others. How did you respond?

305. What Java Web Developer kind of a project/task/ assignment wouldnt you delegate?

306. What s the last, best Java Web Developer business book you have read and what did you learn or applied that learning?

307. How do you ensure others repeat positive behavior?

308. Describe the last time you confronted a peer about something he/she did that bothered you. What were the circumstances?

309. In your last or current Java Web Developer job, what problems did you identify that had previously been

overlooked?

310. What attracts you to this particular Java Web Developer industry?

311. Give an Java Web Developer example of when you had to work with someone who was difficult to get along with. Why was this person difficult?

312. Please give us an Java Web Developer example when you met a tight deadline?

313. What schools have you attended and when?

314. How did you define and measure Java Web Developer success?

315. What achievements from your past work experience are you most proud of?

316. What Java Web Developer things in your job give you a sense of accomplishment?

317. Have you ever had to work with, or for, someone who lied to you in the past?

318. What have been your Java Web Developer experiences in defining long range goals?

319. What Java Web Developer challenges did you face in your last position?

320. What are your Java Web Developer standards of success/goals for a job?

321. What are your short and long-Java Web Developer term goals?

322. Are you in good physical condition?

323. What are some of the books youve read recently?

324. What have you done when your schedule was interrupted on the Java Web Developer job?

325. Have you ever legally changed your name?

326. What if someone on your Java Web Developer team isnt pulling their weight on a project and its affecting the speed and quality of the project...?

327. Have you ever had to manage a Java Web Developer team that was not up to the task?

328. Give an Java Web Developer example of a difficult situation you had with a client or vendor?

329. How much reading of new Java Web Developer information is required in your current job?

330. Tell me about the Java Web Developer system that you use for goal setting. To what extent does it involve using written objectives, paper work or forms?

331. Do you have a list of potential Java Web Developer references?

332. In which Java Web Developer kind of interviews have you participated?

333. Give an Java Web Developer example of a time when you had a conflict with a supervisor?

334. What, in your Java Web Developer opinion, are the key ingredients in guiding and maintaining successful business relationships?

335. What are your major Java Web Developer strengths and weaknesses?

336. How would you describe our organizational Java Web Developer culture?

337. What were your wages at your prior Java Web Developer job?

338. Can you give me a specific Java Web Developer example from your past jobs or other experiences where you had to set priorities and plan your work?

339. Sometimes it is necessary to work in unsettled or rapidly changing circumstances. When have you found yourself in this position?

340. Tell me about a time you saw someone at work stretch or bend the rules beyond what you felt was acceptable. What did you do?

341. Tell me about the biggest risk you ever took?

342. Give an Java Web Developer example to a time when you encountered a difficult situation with a co-worker?

343. Give me a specific Java Web Developer example of a time when you had to work with a difficult customer?

344. Have you ever been in a Java Web Developer situation where, although it was difficult for you, you were honest and told the truth, and suffered negative consequences?

345. Give me an Java Web Developer example of a time at work when you had to deal with unreasonable expectations of you. What parts of your behavior were mature and immature?

346. You come across an online photo of an individual who works for you and his photo has something hanging out of his mouth that certainly looks like a marijuana cigarette Can you fire him?

347. What Are Your Java Web Developer Goals?

348. Whats your nationality?

349. Describe a time when you got co-workers who dislike each other to work together. How did you accomplish this?

350. What led you to select your Java Web Developer college major?

351. Have you ever started something up from nothing – give an Java Web Developer example?

352. What would be the best Java Web Developer example of your ability to be flexible and adaptable?

353. Have you given out any _____?

354. Can you do the Java Web Developer job?

355. What do you know about our Java Web Developer Company and/or the position for which you are applying?

356. What specific Java Web Developer goals, including those related to your occupation, have you established for your life?

357. Give me an Java Web Developer example of a time you had to make an important decision. How did you make the decision?

358. Tell me about a time when your carefully laid plans were fouled up. What happened?

359. How would you feel supervising two or three other Java Web Developer employees?

360. What specific Java Web Developer things did you do to ensure your accuracy?

361. How did you get everything accomplished?

362. What are your areas of strength?

363. Tell me about a Java Web Developer team member from whom it was tough to get cooperation. How did you handle the situation?

364. What type of supervisor works best for you?

365. How long did you serve?

366. Describe a time you had to Java Web Developer delegate parts of a large project or assignment to some of your direct reports. How did you decide what tasks to Java Web Developer delegate to which people?

367. How would you describe the Java Web Developer office culture?

368. What Java Web Developer kind of experience do you have dealing with a heavy workload?

369. List all organizations to which you belong. Were you ever a union Java Web Developer member?

370. Tell me about a time when you were asked to complete a difficult assignment and the odds were against you. What did you learn from the experience?

371. What have you done to remotivate a demoralized Java Web Developer team/person?

372. What Java Web Developer kind of influencing techniques did you use?

373. Whats your typical approach to conflict?

374. When have you been a part of a Java Web Developer team that drove an important business change?

375. What advice do you wish you had been given when

you were starting out?

376. Describe the last time you were criticized by a peer or supervisor. How did you handle it?

377. Provide Java Web Developer examples of when results didn¹t turn out as you planned. What did you do then?

378. What type of position are you looking for?

379. When have you had to cope with the anger or hostility of another person?

380. How would your Java Web Developer manager describe your performance?

381. Can you think of some Java Web Developer projects or ideas that were sold, implemented, or carried out successfully because of your efforts?

382. How will you get to work?

383. Your next question?

384. Tell of some situations in which you have had to adjust quickly to changes over which you had no control. What was the impact of the change on you?

385. How do you determine what is right or fair in delegating Java Web Developer tasks/roles/responsibilities within your organization?

386. How would you describe your interpersonal Java Web Developer communication skills?

387. On a scale of 0-10, how confident are you that you can change successfully?

388. Have you ever managed multiple Java Web Developer projects simultaneously?

389. How did you decide what Java Web Developer tasks to delegate to which people?

390. How often do other Java Web Developer staff treat you the way you want them to?

391. What specific Java Web Developer details should you identify when researching a company?

Believability

1. What do you do differently from other (   )? Why? Give Java Web Developer examples.

2. Give a specific Java Web Developer example of how you have involved subordinates in identifying performance goals and expectations.

3. Give an Java Web Developer example of how you monitor the progress your employees are making on projects or tasks you delegated.

4. What is your Java Web Developer management style? How do you think your subordinates perceive you?

5. All Java Web Developer jobs have their frustrations and problems. Describe some specific tasks or conditions that have been frustrating to you. Why were they frustrating and what did you do?

6. It is important that Java Web Developer performance and other personnel issues be addressed timely. Give examples of the type of personnel issues you've confronted and how you addressed them. Including examples of the process you used for any disciplinary action taken or grievance resolved.

7. What were some of the most important Java Web Developer things you accomplished on your last job?

8. Describe a Java Web Developer situation in which you had to translate a broad or general directive from superiors into individual performance expectations.

How did you do this and what were the results?

9. Describe a Java Web Developer situation in which you received a new procedure or instructions with which you disagreed. What did you do?

10. Sometimes supervisors' evaluations differ from our own. What did you do about it?

11. Java Web Developer Jobs differ in the degree to which unexpected changes can disrupt daily responsibilities. Tell what you did and us about a time when this happened.

12. Give us an Java Web Developer example of when someone brought you a new idea, particularly one that was odd or unusual. What did you do?

13. Describe your ideal supervisor.

14. What are your Java Web Developer standards of success in your job and how do you know when you are successful?

15. We don't always make Java Web Developer decisions that everyone agrees with. Give us an example of an unpopular decision you made. How did you communicate the decision and what was the outcome?

Adaptability

1. How do you know if an Java Web Developer organization is adaptable?

2. Is ours a learning Java Web Developer organization?

3. How do different project Java Web Developer types, procurement routes, clients, and / or locations influence your pull?

4. How does one design for time?

5. What are the licensing, certifications, and credentialing Java Web Developer requirements for this job?

6. Tell me about the first Java Web Developer job you've ever had. What did you do to learn the ropes?

7. Give me an Java Web Developer example of a time when you had to think on your feet in order to delicately extricate yourself from a difficult or awkward situation.

8. Tell me about a time when you failed. Why did it happen? What did you do next and what would you do differently if given another chance?

9. Are you a resilient survivor?

10. How can a hobby prepare you for work?

11. What is your biggest work related Java Web Developer failure in the last six months and how did you overcome it?

12. What other occupations also require your Java Web Developer skills?

13. Describe a time when your Java Web Developer team or company was undergoing some change. How did that impact you, and how did you adapt?

14. What is your greatest Java Web Developer failure, and what did you learn from it?

15. What Java Web Developer benefits do you get from belonging to this organization?

16. What do you do when priorities change quickly? Give one Java Web Developer example of when this happened

17. How would you create and then lead an Java Web Developer organization where the infrastructure is flexible, but yet efficient, effective, and reliable?

18. When the unexpected happens what next?

19. Tell us about a Java Web Developer situation in which you had to adjust to changes over which you had no control. How did you handle it?

20. How many times have you failed?

21. What is your biggest Java Web Developer career screw-up?

22. If you do your Java Web Developer job well, will you automatically get promoted?

23. What Java Web Developer role should a hobby play in this job interview?

24. What was your biggest Java Web Developer failure?

25. What Java Web Developer kinds of educational decisions make you more promotable?

26. In your chosen work Java Web Developer area, what are five careers that seem attractive to you?

27. What is meant by being more flexible?

28. What's your biggest Java Web Developer failure - why is it a Java Web Developer failure and what did you learn from it?

29. Do you have enough stress to make you ill?

30. What is the meaning of Adaptability in the Java Web Developer industry?

31. Tell me about a time you were under a lot of Java Web Developer pressure. What was going on and how did you get through it?

32. Describe a time when you failed to engage at the right level in your Java Web Developer organization. Why did you do that and how did you handle the situation?

33. Describe a major change that occurred in a Java Web Developer job that you held. How did you adapt to this change?

34. In what Java Web Developer ways can you build on your present skills?

35. At what point do you engage/ step away?

36. When does a hobby start to become work?

37. What professional organizations support your careers of interest?

38. What careers would allow you to do what you really enjoy doing?

39. How do we foster a Java Web Developer culture that allows open dialog between everyone regardless of rank?

40. Tell us about a time that you had to adapt to a difficult Java Web Developer situation

41. How do Java Web Developer leaders develop organizations capable of adapting in the volatile, uncertain, complex, and ambiguous environment envisioned by senior Java Web Developer leaders?

42. What ongoing professional Java Web Developer development opportunities exist in this career?

43. Tell me about two memorable Java Web Developer projects, one success and one failure. To what do you attribute the success and failure?

44. Tell me about a time you failed. How did you deal with this Java Web Developer situation?

45. What Java Web Developer skills, activities and attitudes lead to promotion?

46. How must you adapt in your workplace in order to advance?

47. What s the long-Java Web Developer term plan beyond your first job at our company?

48. How might a lateral move help you get the promotion?

Personal Effectiveness

1. Tell us about a time when you took responsibility for an Java Web Developer error and were held personally accountable

2. Tell us about a time when your supervisor criticized your work. How did you respond?

3. It is important to maintain a positive Java Web Developer attitude at work when you have other things on your mind. Give a specific example of when you were able to do that

4. Keeping others informed of your progress/Java Web Developer actions helps them fell comfortable. Tell your methods for keeping your supervisor advised of the status on projects

5. Give an Java Web Developer example of a situation where others were intense but you were able to maintain your composure

6. Tell us about a recent Java Web Developer job or experience that you would describe as a real learning experience? What did you learn from the Java Web Developer job or experience?

7. What have you done to further your own professional Java Web Developer development in the past 5 years

8. When you have been made aware of, or have discovered for yourself, a Java Web Developer problem in your work performance, what was your course of action? Can you give an example?

9. Tell us about some demanding situations in which you managed to remain calm and composed

10. There are times when we are placed under extreme Java Web Developer pressure on the job. Tell about a time when you were under such Java Web Developer pressure and how you handled it

Resolving Conflict

1. Have you ever had to settle conflict between two people on the Java Web Developer job? What was the situation and what did you do?

2. Tell us about a time when you had to help two peers settle a Java Web Developer dispute. How did you go about identifying the issues? What did you do? What was the result?

3. Describe a time when you took personal accountability for a conflict and initiated Java Web Developer contact with the individual(s) involved to explain your actions

4. Have you ever been in a Java Web Developer situation where you had to settle an argument between two friends (or people you knew)? What did you do? What was the result?

Strengths and Weaknesses

1. Tell me about one of the more challenging Java Web Developer projects you've done in your career. What was the goal, and how did you achieve it?

2. What are you good at, and what do you WANT to do?

3. What is the one Java Web Developer word that best describes you?

4. How do you get out of your comfort zone in your Java Web Developer life?

5. Which superhero powers do you value most?

6. Can you please describe a Java Web Developer situation in which you had to overcome some serious obstacles or make some considerable sacrifices to achieve your goal?

7. Why shouldn't I hire you?

8. What are you most proud of?

9. How would you do better?

10. In your professional Java Web Developer career, what is the one thing you are most proud of, and likewise, what's the one thing you are least proud of?

11. If you wouldn't have learned the biggest Java Web Developer lesson you have learned last year, how different your career would be today?

12. At our Java Web Developer company, we believe we can do anything. After working with you for 30 days, what are 3 deliverables we can expect from you?

13. What do you want to be the best in the Java Web Developer world at doing, and why do you want to be known for that?

14. Do you have a chip on your shoulder?

15. What makes you lose track of time and want to work nonstop? Where do you find yourself in 'the flow'?

16. How will you contribute with your work and Java Web Developer skills to make our company reach a specific revenue increase in 3 years?

17. Why should I hire you vs the next person (or robot) to walk through the door?

18. What's the hardest thing you've ever done?

Ambition

1. Describe a project or Java Web Developer idea that was implemented primarily because of your efforts. What was your role? What was the outcome?

2. If you are working now, How is your Java Web Developer job?

3. What Java Web Developer jobs have you had in the past?

4. What supports do you need in getting and keeping a Java Web Developer job?

5. What do we mean by innovation?

6. What are the Java Web Developer key market and consumer trends relevant to our industry?

7. What impact did you have in your last Java Web Developer job?

8. Java Web Developer Ideas for action: how can we press fast forward in innovation?

9. What could you do to impact the metrics that are most relevant to us?

10. What is the most competitive work Java Web Developer situation you have experienced? How did you handle it? What was the result?

11. Are there educational opportunities you need on the Java Web Developer job?

12. What is your sense of how equal men and women are in your field?

13. What are you good at, proud of?

14. How much of your time do you spend doing what you want to do?

15. Is ambition inherently sinful?

16. Tell us about a time when you were particularly effective on prioritizing Java Web Developer tasks and completing a project on schedule

17. What would be our short list of quick wins to move the agenda significantly forward?

18. Describe a time when you made a Java Web Developer suggestion to improve the work in your organization

19. What is the riskiest Java Web Developer decision you have made? What was the situation? What happened?

20. Tell us about a time when you had to go above and beyond the call of duty in order to get a Java Web Developer job done

21. How will you measure Java Web Developer success?

22. How can we deploy existing Java Web Developer knowledge and new, innovative solutions and technologies and make them more readily available to those who need them?

23. What would be the Java Web Developer success criteria for us in the coming years?

24. Would you relocate for a good Java Web Developer job?

25. How can we press fast forward with our people and Java Web Developer skills?

26. Tell us about the last time that you undertook a project that Java Web Developer demanded a lot of initiative

27. Why are science, Java Web Developer technology and innovation essential for the achievement of our Goals?

28. There are times when we work without close Java Web Developer supervision or support to get the job done. Tell us about a time when you found yourself in such a situation and how things turned out

29. Tell us how you keep your Java Web Developer job knowledge current with the on going changes in the industry

30. What are your favorite Java Web Developer things, Java Web Developer things to do and places to go?

31. If you aren t working, what are you doing?

32. What Java Web Developer kinds of jobs interest you?

33. In the Java Web Developer future, how would you prefer to divide your time in any area?

34. What Java Web Developer kinds of challenges did you face on your last job? Give an example of how you handled them

35. What would your best Java Web Developer day / worst Java Web Developer day, look like?

36. What frustrates or bores you?

37. Tell us about a time when a Java Web Developer job had to be completed and you were able to focus your attention and efforts to get it done

38. Which Java Web Developer key barriers to growth can you help to reduce or remove?

39. Which Java Web Developer strategy are you most interested in discussing?

40. What Java Web Developer projects have you started on your own recently? What prompted you to get started?

41. Are you looking for opportunity for growth and advancement on the Java Web Developer job?

42. When you disagree with your Java Web Developer manager, what do you do? Give an example

43. Who buys our Java Web Developer product and services and why?

44. What Java Web Developer relationships, if any, exist

between your self-confidence and ambition?

45. How many Java Web Developer hours a day do you put into your work? What were your study patterns at school?

46. Give two Java Web Developer examples of things you've done in previous jobs that demonstrate your willingness to work hard

47. Give an Java Web Developer example of an important goal that you set in the past. Tell about your success in reaching it

48. What Java Web Developer sorts of things have you done to become better qualified for your career?

49. When you have a lot of work to do, how do you get it all done? Give an Java Web Developer example?

50. What do others say about you?

51. What was the best Java Web Developer idea that you came up with in your career? How did you apply it?

52. How collectively can we make a measurable Java Web Developer difference?

53. Java Web Developer Ideas for action: how can we press fast forward in our markets?

54. Are there any barriers to your employment?

55. What did you learn from where you've been, past experience?

56. Is there anything else I need to learn to move forward?

Removing Obstacles

1. What have you done to help your subordinates to be more productive?

2. What have you done to make sure that your subordinates can be productive? Give an Java Web Developer example

3. What do you do when a subordinate comes to you with a challenge?

4. Have you ever dealt with a Java Web Developer situation where communications were poor? Where there was a lack of cooperation? Lack of trust? How did you handle these Java Web Developer situations?

Index

author 1, 39
authority   35, 52, 119, 139, 181, 189, 267
automate   66
available   292
average   55, 99
avoided   63
awkward   281
background   28, 36, 187, 219, 221, 250, 253
balance   25, 84, 200, 260
balancing   144
bankers   99
barbers   97
bargain   87, 133
barriers 20, 27, 63, 294-295
battle 39
Beatles 67
became   10, 71
because   31, 60, 106-107, 125, 152, 277, 291
become   13, 71, 77, 94, 120, 142, 174-175, 206, 218, 249, 284, 295
becomes   181
becoming   217
before 10, 18, 22, 41, 64, 111, 116, 155, 159, 192, 195, 199, 202, 206, 217-218, 229, 248
beginning   150
begins 178
behavior   3, 242, 246, 248, 268, 270, 274
Behavioral   70, 242, 251
behaviors   48, 155
behind 40
belief 248
beliefs 55, 250
believe25, 35, 37, 140, 156, 180, 231, 290
believed   255
belong 151, 154, 256, 276
belonging   282
beneath   221
benefit 1, 95, 224
benefits   25, 100, 147, 149, 206, 282
besides   78, 87
better 25, 30, 92, 142, 175, 195, 226, 229, 235, 248, 250, 260, 289, 295

honest 49, 246, 274
honorable   245
honorably   242
hostile 169
hostility 10, 277
hour-hand   95, 100
household   244
Humility   24
Hunger 24
identical   96-97
identified   1, 10, 20, 204
identify 28, 37, 79, 86, 88, 147, 164, 171, 196, 265, 270, 278
illegal   190, 212
illustrate   11
imaginary   27
immature   274
immediate   243
immoral   190
impact 55, 125, 130, 277, 282, 291
impacted   13, 74, 192, 244
impacts   126, 179
impatient   71, 214
implement   32-33, 37, 120, 138, 163
important   7, 14, 29, 36, 38, 41, 44-46, 49, 55, 58, 60-61, 63,
66, 72, 78, 82-83, 102-104, 106-107, 119, 124, 127, 132, 135-136,
141, 145, 164-165, 175, 178, 180, 186, 190, 196, 198-199, 205, 216,
221, 234, 238, 243, 248, 266, 275-276, 279, 286, 295
imposed   201
impression   165
impressive   196
improve   7, 30, 44, 66, 80, 113, 119, 121, 123, 126, 129, 156,
168-169, 198, 215, 225, 227, 257, 260, 292
improved   11, 114, 116-117
improving   175, 255
incentives   178
incidents   94
included   262
Including   275, 279
increase   87, 175, 181, 200, 231, 290
increases   179
increasing   31
incredible   212
incredibly   24

percentage   147, 212
perfect   187, 265
perform   95, 142, 158, 230, 235, 260
performed   120, 129, 150
performers   208, 218, 231
period 81, 230, 255
permission   1, 219
person 1, 11, 13, 24, 35, 41, 43-45, 48-49, 52-53, 55-56, 64, 67, 71-72, 80-81, 98, 100, 124-126, 129, 136, 142, 159, 167, 181, 194, 206-207, 227, 242, 246, 252-253, 255, 260, 264, 271, 276-277, 290
personal   3, 13, 16, 25, 29-30, 39, 54, 77, 84, 131, 136, 149, 159, 183, 226, 228, 231-232, 249, 259-260, 268, 286, 288
personally   38, 44-45, 163, 249, 286
personnel   279
persons   250
persuade   36-38, 46, 124, 135, 140, 265
persuaded   44, 248
persuading   117, 175
persuasion   2, 7, 35
persuasive   35, 248
Peters 40
petrol 98
philosophy   149, 156, 160
physical   158, 187, 242, 272
picked 171
picture 13, 19, 61, 81, 83, 186, 254
piecemeal   90
placed98, 287
places 214, 293
planned   137, 162, 166, 197, 246, 260, 277
planning   2-3, 86, 153, 155, 166, 184, 194, 246, 256-257
played 104, 132, 171, 180
player 77
players 32
Please 24-25, 34, 61, 99, 103, 123, 128, 132, 164, 270-271, 289
pleased   7, 123, 165, 269
pleasure   188
points 159, 202, 224, 244, 265
policies   51, 122, 139, 151, 221
policy 7, 31, 37, 65, 111, 123, 134, 143, 151, 155, 163, 187, 218, 245, 263
political   58, 268
politics 268

Made in the USA
Monee, IL
04 June 2022